Lily Frend. — Own Book from Home.
Miss Sonnex Class

MY TOP PREDATORS
GOLDEN EAGLE
MY TOP PREDATORS
SOLIFUGE
MY TOP PREDATORS
HORNED FROG
MY TOP PREDATORS
EYELASH VIPER
MY TOP PREDATORS
SPOTTED HYAENA
MY TOP PREDATORS
LEOPARD SEAL
MY TOP PREDATORS
FLOWER MANTIS
MY TOP PREDATORS
AFRICAN WILD DOG
MY TOP PREDATORS
GANNET
MY TOP PREDATORS
LEAST WEASEL

SPOTTED HYAENA
WEAPONS 12
Massive crunching jaws and teeth, strong legs and claws, group cooperation
SIZE 13
Male 1.6 m, female up to 1.8 m
DANGER TO HUMANS 8
May bite, usually retreats
LIFESPAN 8
10–12 years
Kills as much food as it scavenges, very persistent, but has difficulty when prey are fit and well and difficult to catch.
EXPERT 8 RATING
EYELASH VIPER
WEAPONS 14
Long stabbing fangs that inject poison
SIZE 8
80 cm
DANGER TO HUMANS 12
Bites in self-defence, venom rarely fatal
LIFESPAN 6
8–12 years
Excellent senses include heat-detecting pit organs, but fairly small in size, not that muscular, and limited to hunting at night.
EXPERT 9 RATING
HORNED FROG
WEAPONS 3
Big, wide, tough-skinned mouth, skin poison deters enemies
SIZE 4
Male 18 cm, female 22 cm
DANGER TO HUMANS 4
Possible rash from touching skin
LIFESPAN 1
4-6 years
Good camouflage, able to stay still for hours then suddenly lunge, but cannot cope with dryness, slow when conditions are cool.
EXPERT 19 RATING
SOLIFUGE
WEAPONS 4
Great fangs, strong legs to hold prey
SIZE 2
Body up to 10 cm
DANGER TO HUMANS 11
Venom painful but not deadly
LIFESPAN 4
10-plus years
Rapid sprint speed, excellent reactions, but some senses are limited, and dislikes bright light so usually limited to night hunt ng.
EXPERT 17 RATING
GOLDEN EAGLE
WEAPONS 8
Long, sharp talons on powerful feet, sharply hooked beak
SIZE 10
1 m
DANGER TO HUMANS 3
No significant danger
LIFESPAN 18
30–plus years
Excellent senses and flying ability, but lives in habitats where suitable prey may be very scarce for long periods.
EXPERT 11 RATING
LEAST WEASEL
WEAPONS 1
Small but sharp teeth and claws
SIZE 5
Male 23 cm, female 19 cm
DANGER TO HUMANS 5
May bite in self-defence
LIFESPAN 2
5–6 years
Exceptionally fast and agile, slim body to get into burrows and crevices, but needs lots of food to stay warm and active.
EXPERT 18 RATING
GANNET
WEAPONS 15
Strong, dagger-like beak, ideally shaped for seizing fish and squid
SIZE 9
87–100 cm
DANGER TO HUMANS 6
Could do serious damage with its sharp beak
LIFESPAN 15
16–21 years
This super-streamlined bird is perfectly adapted for life as a high-speed diving predator.
EXPERT 7 RATING
AFRICAN WILD DOG
WEAPONS 7
Big teeth and jaws, strong claws, group cooperation
SIZE 11
Head-body 90 cm, tail 35 cm
DANGER TO HUMANS 7
Rarely bites, usually backs off
LIFESPAN 9
12–18 years
Amazing stamina, good senses and running speed, but lives in difficult habitats where prey is scarce, not great reactions.
EXPERT 15 RATING
FLOWER MANTIS
WEAPONS 2
Spiny front legs, huge eyes, strong, sharp mouthparts
SIZE 1
4–5 cm
DANGER TO HUMANS 1
No danger other than prickly spikes
LIFESPAN 3
5 years
Tremendous camouflage and lightning reactions, but limited to sit-and-wait, not good at foraging for prey.
EXPERT 20 RATING
LEOPARD SEAL
WEAPONS 13
Long, wide jaws, sharp teeth, good strength and agility
SIZE 17
Male 3.4 m, female up to 3.8 m
DANGER TO HUMANS 15
One recorded human death
LIFESPAN 16
22–28 years
Extremely fast and agile in water, good sight and detection of water currents, but is up against very fast, manoeuvrable prey.
EXPERT 6 RATING

MY TOP PREDATORS
MY TOP PREDATORS
ROCK PYTHON
MY TOP PREDATORS
WHALE
TIGER
MY TOP PREDATORS
EAGLE OWL
MY TOP PREDATORS
BARRACUDA
MY TOP PREDATORS
RED-BELLIED PIRANHA
MY TOP PREDATORS
NILE CROCODILE
MY TOP PREDATORS
HUNTSMAN SPIDER
MY TOP PREDATORS
POLAR BEAR

EAGLE OWL
WEAPONS 6
Strong legs and feet with sharp talons, narrow knife-sharp beak
SIZE 7
75 cm
DANGER TO HUMANS 2
No significant danger
LIFESPAN 12
15–20 years
Supreme night hunter, amazing sight and even better hearing, quiet flight, but many of its victims also have well-tuned senses.
EXPERT 16 RATING
TIGER
WEAPONS 18
Big claws, long teeth, great strength
SIZE 15
Head-body up to 2.5 m, tail up to 1 m
DANGER TO HUMANS 18
Very dangerous, can turn man-eater
LIFESPAN 13
10–20 years
As a top predator, the tiger can kill most victims, but for hunting efficiency it needs prey big enough to be a worthwhile feed.
EXPERT 5 RATING
KILLER WHALE
WEAPONS 16
Enormous size and power, strong jaws and teeth, pack cooperation
SIZE 20
Male up to 9 m, female 8 m
DANGER TO HUMANS 16
Hardly any recorded attacks
LIFESPAN 20
Up to 60 years, rarely 80-plus
Massive strength, stamina, speed, good coordination and intelligence, but not very agile when chasing fast, darting prey.
EXPERT 2 RATING
ROCK PYTHON
WEAPONS 17
Big jaws and teeth, muscular body for squeezing
SIZE 19
6 m, exceptionally more
DANGER TO HUMANS 17
Dangerous, has eaten several humans
LIFESPAN 17
25-plus years
Great camouflage, good smell and vibration detection, extending jaws, but large bulk means slow in cold conditions.
EXPERT 3 RATING
GREY WOLF
WEAPONS 10
Stamina, strong claws, large canine teeth, group cooperation
SIZE 14
Nose to tail-tip 2 m
DANGER TO HUMANS 10
May bite but rarely serious
LIFESPAN 6
8-12 years
Good senses, wide diet, brings down large prey as a pack, but has problems catching enough small victims when hunting alone.
EXPERT 10 RATING
POLAR BEAR
WEAPONS 19
Huge paws and claws, strong bite
SIZE 16
Male up to 3 m, female 2.5 m
DANGER TO HUMANS 19
Very dangerous, attacks often fatal
LIFESPAN 14
20 years
Powerful top predator, excellent senses and stalk technique, but its specialized environment – sea ice – can vary greatly.
EXPERT 4 RATING
HUNTSMAN SPIDER
WEAPONS 9
Strong legs, sharp, poisonous fangs
SIZE 3
Head-body 11-12 cm
DANGER TO HUMANS 13
Venom painful, deaths very rare
LIFESPAN 11
15-plus years
A stealth stalker with a fast final lunge and enough poison to subdue smaller prey, but vulnerable when out in the open.
EXPERT 13 RATING
NILE CROCODILE
WEAPONS 20
Massive jaws, plentiful teeth, great bite power
SIZE 18
Male up to 5.5 m, female 4 m
DANGER TO HUMANS 20
Very dangerous, many human deaths
LIFESPAN 19
50-plus years
Good camouflage, great swimmer, stealthy ambush technique, but senses could be better, slow reactions in cold conditions.
EXPERT 1 RATING
RED-BELLIED PIRANHA
WEAPONS 11
Razor-sharp triangular teeth, strong jaws
SIZE 6
30–40 cm
DANGER TO HUMANS 14
Mass attack by shoal can be fatal
LIFESPAN 6
8-12 years
Good eyesight and other senses, smallish and manoeuvrable, but hunts in difficult cloudy-water habitats with many obstructions.
EXPERT 12 RATING
BARRACUDA
WEAPONS 5
Darting speed, long fangs, fast sprint swimmer
SIZE 12
Up to 1.8 m
DANGER TO HUMANS 9
Attacks rare, bites not serious
LIFESPAN 10
10–15 years
Good senses for the habitat, but specialized for deep-water conditions where prey is very scarce, not very agile, little stamina.
EXPERT 14 RATING

MY TOP EXTREME ANIMALS
GALAPAGOS MARINE IGUANA
MY TOP EXTREME ANIMALS
EMPEROR PENGUIN
MY TOP EXTREME ANIMALS
ELEPHANT SEAL
MY TOP EXTREME ANIMALS
CHEETAH
MY TOP EXTREME ANIMALS
ARMY ANT
MY TOP EXTREME ANIMALS
OSTRICH
MY TOP EXTREME ANIMALS
LESSER FLAMINGO
MY TOP EXTREME ANIMALS
JAPANESE MACAQUE
MY TOP EXTREME ANIMALS
BLACK-THROATED HUMMINGBIRD
MY TOP EXTREME ANIMALS
GIRAFFE

ARMY ANT

SIZE 1
Workers 5–10 mm, soldiers 20-plus mm

LIFESPAN 5
Workers 3–12 months, queens 10-plus years

EXTREME FEATURES 8
Huge jaws for size, stinging spray, enormous numbers

LIMITS 1
Small and weak on their own

Army ants are only powerful when they attack together as a huge group, and they must keep on the move.

EXPERT RATING 19

CHEETAH

SIZE 14
Head-body 1.2 m, tail 80 cm

LIFESPAN 6
10–12 years

EXTREME FEATURES 19
Fastest land animal, amazing acceleration, very agile

LIMITS 6
Runs out of stamina and overheats after a minute's sprint

The cheetah cannot sustain its speed and must catch its prey fast, before it becomes breathless and its muscles overheat.

EXPERT RATING 11

ELEPHANT SEAL

SIZE 18
Male 6 m, female 3 m

LIFESPAN 15
Male 20 years, female 25 years

EXTREME FEATURES 18
Huge size and power, makes very long, deep dives

LIMITS 19
Fights between males at breeding time cause serious wounds

The biggest seal has little to fear from natural enemies, even killer whales, but it needs huge amounts of food.

EXPERT RATING 2

EMPEROR PENGUIN

SIZE 12
1.2 m

LIFESPAN 14
20–25 years, rarely 40–plus

EXTREME FEATURES 17
Copes with the coldest conditions on Earth

LIMITS 20
Blizzards can prevent it reaching the sea to feed

The male emperor penguin must rely on stored body fat for more than two months in the world's worst conditions.

EXPERT RATING 3

GALAPAGOS MARINE IGUANA

SIZE 13
Male up to 1.5 m, female 1 m

LIFESPAN 11
20 years

EXTREME FEATURES 7
Dives well, eats varied seaweeds

LIMITS 10
May get too chilled to leave the sea

This lizard has plenty of seashore food, but it has to bask in the sunshine regularly, or it gets too cold to move.

EXPERT RATING 13

GIRAFFE

SIZE 18
Male 5.5 m, female 4.5 m

LIFESPAN 13
20–25 years

EXTREME FEATURES 14
Amazing long neck and legs to reach high-up food

LIMITS 8
Awkward when stooping to drink

The giraffe feeds higher in trees than any other animal, but it's at risk of tripping and injuring its spindly legs.

EXPERT RATING 6

BLACK-THROATED HUMMINGBIRD

SIZE 2
10 cm

LIFESPAN 3
5–7 years

EXTREME FEATURES 6
Very fast wing beats, extraordinary agility in the air

LIMITS 7
Needs lots of high-energy food

Hummingbirds use so much energy when flying that they must feed often through the day or they starve.

EXPERT RATING 18

JAPANESE MACAQUE

SIZE 9
Head-body 70 cm, tail 10 cm

LIFESPAN 16
25–30 years

EXTREME FEATURES 12
Thick fur, survives very cold weather, intelligent

LIMITS 17
Difficult to find food in winter

This smart, inventive monkey takes advantage of many kinds of foods depending on season and habitat.

EXPERT RATING 5

LESSER FLAMINGO

SIZE 10
90–100 cm

LIFESPAN 19
Up to 50 years

EXTREME FEATURES 6
Very long, bendy neck, stilt-like legs

LIMITS 7
Legs are fragile and easily injured

The flamingo has very specialized food requirements and cannot adapt to other habitats or food sources.

EXPERT RATING 12

OSTRICH

SIZE 15
2–2.2 m

LIFESPAN 18
40 years, rarely more

EXTREME FEATURES 11
Long, bendy neck, very powerful legs, fast runner

LIMITS 16
Needs more water and shade than many other desert dwellers

The ostrich has great speed and stamina, able to race away in escape or trot long distances to find fresh food.

EXPERT RATING 4

MY TOP WEIRD ANIMALS
JACKSON'S CHAMELEON
MY TOP WEIRD ANIMALS
PORCUPINEFISH
MY TOP WEIRD ANIMALS
AARDVARK
MY TOP WEIRD ANIMALS
PEACOCK MANTIS SHRIMP
MY TOP WEIRD ANIMALS
SHORT-BEAKED ECHIDNA
MY TOP WEIRD ANIMALS
GOLDENROD CRAB SPIDER
MY TOP WEIRD ANIMALS
GIRAFFE WEEVIL
MY TOP WEIRD ANIMALS
KNOBBED HORNBILL
MY TOP WEIRD ANIMALS
FRILLED LIZARD
MY TOP WEIRD ANIMALS
VAMPIRE BAT

SHORT-BEAKED ECHIDNA

SIZE 12

40–45 cm

LIFESPAN 19

40–45 years

WEIRD FEATURES 18

Lays eggs, strong spines, slender snout

THREATS 11

Preyed on by big snakes, lizards and dingoes; introduced predators, habitat loss

The echidna leads a secretive life well-protected by its stout, sharp spines, and is rarely bothered by enemies.

EXPERT RATING 4

PEACOCK MANTIS SHRIMP

SIZE 9

Up to 25 cm

LIFESPAN 7

Possibly 5–10 years

WEIRD FEATURES 8

Hammer-like front legs, large eyes

THREATS 12

Preyed on by big fish, octopus, seals; pollution, global warming, fishing

It can deliver one of the quickest, strongest attacks of any animal, so other creatures avoid this large, fierce shrimp.

EXPERT RATING 14

AARDVARK

SIZE 20

2 m

LIFESPAN 13

10–15 years

WEIRD FEATURES 5

Huge, long nose, big long ears

THREATS 5

Preyed on by lions, leopards, hyaenas; hunted by humans for meat

Aardvarks have brilliant senses of smell and hearing, and dig extra-fast with their big claws to hide from enemies.

EXPERT RATING 11

PORCUPINEFISH

SIZE 8

20 cm

LIFESPAN 8

Unknown in the wild, possibly 5–10 years

WEIRD FEATURES 9

Swells up with swallowed water, sharp spines

THREATS 13

Preyed on by larger fish, octopus; pollution, coral bleaching

Most predators seem to find the porcupinefish too tricky to eat, so it is rarely threatened by other animals.

EXPERT RATING 13

JACKSON'S CHAMELEON

SIZE 10

30 cm

LIFESPAN 4

3–5 years

WEIRD FEATURES 14

Long, sticky tongue, horns, camouflage

THREATS 16

Preyed on by birds of prey, snakes, wild cats; habitat loss, captured for pet trade

Male chameleons show off their horns, then flick out their long tongues at lightning speed to catch a meal.

EXPERT RATING 10

VAMPIRE BAT

SIZE 6

9 cm

LIFESPAN 10

8–11 years

WEIRD FEATURES 3

Drinks only blood, ultra-sharp teeth

THREATS 3

Preyed on by bigger bats, owls, wild cats; domestic animal diseases

Blood must contain all the nutrients necessary for life because this bat feeds on nothing else. It's also very agile on the ground.

EXPERT RATING 16

FRILLED LIZARD

SIZE 19

90 cm

LIFESPAN 12

10–15 years

WEIRD FEATURES 10

Large neck frill, can stand up on back legs

THREATS 9

Preyed on by big snakes and lizards, birds of prey, dingoes; habitat loss

The frilled lizard's defence display – flapping, hissing and dancing – is one of the most bizarre examples of animal behaviour.

EXPERT RATING 8

KNOBBED HORNBILL

SIZE 18

80–90 cm

LIFESPAN 17

25–30 years

WEIRD FEATURES 6

Huge beak, bright colours, walled-in nest

THREATS 14

Preyed on by snakes, wild cats, birds of prey; habitat loss, trophy hunters

Despite the beak's massive size, the hornbill uses it with great accuracy to pick up tiny berries and seeds.

EXPERT RATING 6

GIRAFFE WEEVIL

SIZE 4

Up to 3 cm

LIFESPAN 2

Unknown, probably 1–2 years

WEIRD FEATURES 13

Extraordinary long neck

THREATS 4

Preyed on by many creatures, from spiders and mantises to shrews and birds

The weird neck is part of breeding success, with the longest-necked males able to mate with the most females.

EXPERT RATING 15

GOLDENROD CRAB SPIDER

SIZE 2

Up to 11 mm

LIFESPAN 5

Unknown, possibly 5 years

WEIRD FEATURES 7

Amazing camouflage, sideways movement

THREATS 1

Preyed on by many creatures, from big spiders to bats and birds

Able to change its colour gradually to match its flower exactly, there are few better examples of animal camouflage.

EXPERT RATING 19

MY TOP WEIRD ANIMALS
PLATYPUS
MY TOP WEIRD ANIMALS
THREE-BANDED ARMADILLO
MY TOP WEIRD ANIMALS
POT-BELLY SEAHORSE
MY TOP WEIRD ANIMALS
TRYON'S SEA SLUG
MY TOP WEIRD ANIMALS
NAKED MOLE RAT
MY TOP WEIRD ANIMALS
PROBOSCIS MONKEY
MY TOP WEIRD ANIMALS
STALK-EYED FLY
MY TOP WEIRD ANIMALS
HOATZIN
MY TOP WEIRD ANIMALS
TUATARA
MY TOP WEIRD ANIMALS
ECUADOR TREE FROG

NAKED MOLE RAT

SIZE 7
Up to 12 cm

LIFESPAN 18
Up to 28 years

WEIRD FEATURES 17
'Queen' rules colony, almost no fur

THREATS 7
Preyed on by snakes and wild cats; rivalries with other mole rat colonies, habitat loss

The mole rat colony is organized more like an insect nest, with one queen and lots of non-breeding workers.

EXPERT 9 RATING

TRYON'S SEA SLUG

SIZE 5
6 cm

LIFESPAN 3
Unknown, possibly 1–2 years

WEIRD FEATURES 2
Glowing colours, frilly gills

THREATS 10
Preyed on by fish, crabs, starfish; pollution, fishing, coral destruction

Sea slugs do not need to rush since their luminous colours tell other creatures that their flesh is poisonous.

EXPERT 17 RATING

POT-BELLY SEAHORSE

SIZE 11
35 cm

LIFESPAN 9
Up to 10 years

WEIRD FEATURES 4
Tiny mouth, prehensile tail, male 'gives birth'

THREATS 18
Preyed on by bigger fish, squid, seals; fishing, pet collectors

For survival, seahorses rely on hiding, camouflage and hard bony plates in the skin – they are too slow to escape.

EXPERT 12 RATING

THREE-BANDED ARMADILLO

SIZE 13
45–50 cm

LIFESPAN 14
15 years

WEIRD FEATURES 12
Armour plating, can roll into a ball

THREATS 19
Preyed on by mountain lions, jaguars, crocs and caimans; habitat loss

The armadillo is very adaptable, able to eat most foods, and almost no predators can harm it when it's rolled up.

EXPERT 5 RATING

PLATYPUS

SIZE 14
Up to 50 cm in length

LIFESPAN 11
10–15 years

WEIRD FEATURES 19
Beak, broad tail, lays eggs, webbed feet

THREATS 8
Preyed on by snakes and lizards; introduced predators, water pollution

The strange platypus is like a made-up creature constructed from odd bits of different mammals, plus some bird features.

EXPERT 7 RATING

ECUADOR TREE FROG

SIZE 3
2–3 cm

LIFESPAN 6
Unknown, possibly 4–6 years

WEIRD FEATURES 1
Huge eyes, extra-long back legs, sucker toes

THREATS 6
Preyed on by lizards, snakes, birds of prey; habitat destruction

Tree frogs need very big eyes to see food such as tiny flies in the gloom of their rainforest habitat.

EXPERT 18 RATING

TUATARA

SIZE 15
Up to 60 cm

LIFESPAN 20
Can exceed 100 years

WEIRD FEATURES 20
Grows very slowly, 'third eye', long hibernation

THREATS 17
Preyed on by seabirds; introduced species such as rats, habitat loss

Not a true lizard, the tuatara has one of the longest animal life cycles – even its eggs take over a year to hatch.

EXPERT 1 RATING

HOATZIN

SIZE 17
60–70 cm

LIFESPAN 16
20–25 years

WEIRD FEATURES 16
Chick's wing claws, tiny head, poor flier

THREATS 15
Preyed on by wild cats, birds of prey, snakes; habitat loss, pollution

The hoatzin looks like a cartoon throwback to the dinosaur age yet manages well in its rainforest home.

EXPERT 3 RATING

STALK-EYED FLY

SIZE 1
Up to 1 cm

LIFESPAN 1
Mostly a few months

WEIRD FEATURES 11
Big eyes on very long stalks

THREATS 2
Preyed on by many creatures from dragonflies to spiders, lizards, birds and bats

The long stalks and heavy eyes can cause balance problems when flying fast to escape from predators.

EXPERT 20 RATING

PROBOSCIS MONKEY

SIZE 16
Up to 70 cm

LIFESPAN 15
Unknown, probably 20 years

WEIRD FEATURES 15
Large nose, feeds only from mangrove trees

THREATS 20
Preyed on by tigers, leopards, crocodiles; habitat loss, pollution, hunting

The nose is longest in older males, and mangrove trees provide all this monkey's foods and other needs.

EXPERT 2 RATING

MY TOP ANIMAL GIANTS
KOMODO DRAGON
MY TOP ANIMAL GIANTS
LION'S MANE JELLYFISH
MY TOP ANIMAL GIANTS
GIANT COCONUT CRAB
MY TOP ANIMAL GIANTS
BISON
MY TOP ANIMAL GIANTS
MOUNTAIN GORILLA
MY TOP ANIMAL GIANTS
WANDERING ALBATROSS
MY TOP ANIMAL GIANTS
SALTWATER CROCODILE
MY TOP ANIMAL GIANTS
MANTA RAY
MY TOP ANIMAL GIANTS
GIANT AFRICAN LAND SNAIL
MY TOP ANIMAL GIANTS
PACIFIC GIANT OCTOPUS

MOUNTAIN GORILLA

GIANT FEATURES 13
Strong bulky body and long strong arms

SIZE 8
Male up to 1.8 m, female 1.5 m

DANGER TO HUMANS 15
Only attacks if threatened but then extremely dangerous

LIFESPAN 13
About 35 years in the wild

The gorilla is the biggest and strongest of all the primates. The male is more than twice the weight of an average adult man.

EXPERT 7 RATING

BISON

GIANT FEATURES 15
Massive head and horns of up to 61 cm in length

SIZE 13
Head-body up to 3.5 m, tail 60 cm

DANGER TO HUMANS 17
Very dangerous if you get too close

LIFESPAN 8
12–20 years

The biggest land animal in North America, the bison is a surprisingly fast runner.

EXPERT 6 RATING

GIANT COCONUT CRAB

GIANT FEATURES 2
Huge claws for breaking open coconuts and other food

SIZE 4
1-m legspan

DANGER TO HUMANS 4
Too slow moving to be a real danger but could give a nasty nip if you get too close

LIFESPAN 14
Up to 40 years

The largest land crab, this crustacean does not have a hard shell but does grow a tough skin over itself.

EXPERT 18 RATING

LION'S MANE JELLYFISH

GIANT FEATURES 8
Tentacles up to 30 m long and lined with stinging cells

SIZE 10
Bell up to 2 m across

DANGER TO HUMANS 8
Tentacles cause painful but not fatal wounds

LIFESPAN 2
About 1 year

The largest known jellyfish, this creature uses its huge bunches of long slender tentacles to catch fish and shellfish.

EXPERT 16 RATING

KOMODO DRAGON

GIANT FEATURES 6
Big mouth and serrated teeth up to 2.5 cm long

SIZE 12
3 m

DANGER TO HUMANS 16
Very dangerous and has a venomous bite

LIFESPAN 11
About 30 years

The biggest living lizards, Komodos are large fierce animals with a deadly bite, and will eat any prey they encounter.

EXPERT 9 RATING

PACIFIC GIANT OCTOPUS

GIANT FEATURES 9
Eight long arms each lined with 260 suction cups

SIZE 15
5 m

DANGER TO HUMANS 5
Does not attack humans but will defend its den against any diver who gets too close

LIFESPAN 3
About 4 years

The world's largest octopus, this animal is believed to be the most intelligent of all invertebrates.

EXPERT 14 RATING

GIANT AFRICAN LAND SNAIL

GIANT FEATURES 1
Shell is up to 20 cm – longer than an adult human's hand

SIZE 2
Up to 30 cm with body extended

DANGER TO HUMANS 2
None, but it does eat farmers' crops

LIFESPAN 4
Up to 9 years

The world's largest snail, this is also a fast breeder so spreads very fast – even where it is not wanted.

EXPERT 20 RATING

MANTA RAY

GIANT FEATURES 7
Huge winglike fins help this fish to power through the water

SIZE 18
Up to 7 m

DANGER TO HUMANS 6
Not dangerous to humans unless disturbed, when it can lash out with its tail

LIFESPAN 9
About 20 years

Despite its size, this huge fish feeds only on small planktonic creatures that it filters from the water.

EXPERT 10 RATING

SALTWATER CROCODILE

GIANT FEATURES 17
Huge powerful jaws and strong teeth for tearing prey apart

SIZE 17
6 m

DANGER TO HUMANS 19
Very dangerous indeed, has killed a large number of people

LIFESPAN 18
About 70 years

The biggest of the crocodiles, this fierce hunter can catch animals as large as buffalo.

EXPERT 2 RATING

WANDERING ALBATROSS

GIANT FEATURES 16
Huge wings measuring 3.4 m from tip to tip

SIZE 5
1.1 m

DANGER TO HUMANS 3
Rarely comes into contact with humans but could give a nasty bite with its hooked beak

LIFESPAN 11
30 years

With the largest wingspan of any bird, this albatross is a champion flyer and glides long distances with scarcely a wing beat.

EXPERT 12 RATING

MY TOP SHARKS
MEGAMO
SHARK
MY TOP SHARKS
SAND TI
SHARK
MY TOP SHARKS
SPINY DOGFISH
MY TOP SHARKS
BAMBOO SHARK
MY TOP SHARKS
PORT JACKSON SHARK
MY TOP SHARKS
SWELLSHARK
MY TOP SHARKS
TIGER SHA
MY TOP SHARKS
WHALE SHARK
MY TOP SHARKS
SPOTTED WOBBEGONG
WHITETIP REEF SHARK

PORT JACKSON SHARK
SIZE 4
Up to 1.5 m
LIFESPAN 12
Unknown, perhaps 30 years
DANGER TO HUMANS 8
May cause minimal harm if severely provoked
THREATS 3
Bigger predatory fish, pollution, fishing trawls, spearfishing
Coastal pollution and increased fishing for its shellfish prey are having bad effects on this usually timid shark.
EXPERT 16 RATING
BAMBOO SHARK
SIZE 2
1 m
LIFESPAN 3
Unknown, possibly 15–20 years
DANGER TO HUMANS 7
Usually harmless, may give a warning nip
THREATS 11
Habitat loss, pollution, overfishing, bigger predatory fish
Damage to coral reefs and similar habitats due to global warming and pollution is greatly affecting this shark.
EXPERT 19 RATING
SPINY DOGFISH
SIZE 1
Up to 1 m
LIFESPAN 15
35-plus years
DANGER TO HUMANS 12
Poison spines inflict very painful injuries
THREATS 19
Trawl nets, pollution, bigger predatory fish, dolphins, seals
With its wide diet, this small shark was once very common, but intensive fishing means it has become rare in many places.
EXPERT 6 RATING
SAND TIGER SHARK
SIZE 8
3 m
LIFESPAN 4
15–20 years
DANGER TO HUMANS 16
Powerful if provoked, fatalities rare
THREATS 18
Fishing nets, spearfishing, pollution, killer whales
Fishing for fins, oil and flesh, coastal pollution and revenge killings by people are all making this shark more rare.
EXPERT 10 RATING
MEGAMOUTH SHARK
SIZE 16
5.5 m
LIFESPAN 19
Unknown, possibly 100 years
DANGER TO HUMANS 6
None – too rare, too deep, no big teeth
THREATS 1
Deep-sea trawl nets, submarine sonar, sperm whales
With only about 50 good sightings, little is known about this monster of the deep, but it may be more common than once thought.
EXPERT 12 RATING
WHITETIP REEF SHARK
SIZE 6
Up to 2 m
LIFESPAN 2
20-plus years
DANGER TO HUMANS 9
May bite if provoked, no deaths
THREATS 10
Pollution, habitat loss, bigger predatory fish
The whitetip will probably become more at risk as fishing fleets turn to it after fishing out other sharks.
EXPERT 18 RATING
SPOTTED WOBBEGONG
SIZE 7
3 m
LIFESPAN 14
Unknown, possibly 30-plus years
DANGER TO HUMANS 14
Bite injuries can be serious, no fatalities
THREATS 9
Bottom trawling, pollution, habitat loss
Inshore pollution and sea bed trawling mean the wobbegong's habitats are slowly being destroyed.
EXPERT 11 RATING
WHALE SHARK
SIZE 20
Up to 12 m
LIFESPAN 18
70-plus years
DANGER TO HUMANS 3
Peaceful, occasional butting or collisions
THREATS 15
Boat collisions, killer whales, fishing nets
Largest of all fish, the whale shark is harmless to humans, but not the other way around – its fins make prized soup.
EXPERT 3 RATING
TIGER SHARK
SIZE 15
4.5 m
LIFESPAN 11
25-plus years
DANGER TO HUMANS 18
In the 'Big Three', attacks and kills suddenly
THREATS 8
Plastics and similar pollution, sports anglers, nets, killer whales
Tiger sharks snap at almost any object and some die after swallowing human trash such as plastic bags that block their guts.
EXPERT 5 RATING
SWELL SHARK
SIZE 3
1 m
LIFESPAN 10
Unknown, possibly 20–30 years
DANGER TO HUMANS 11
No recorded serious injuries
THREATS 2
Bigger predatory fish, nets and trawls, seals
The main human threat is bycatch – accidental trapping in nets, trawls and traps meant for other creatures such as shellfish.
EXPERT 17 RATING

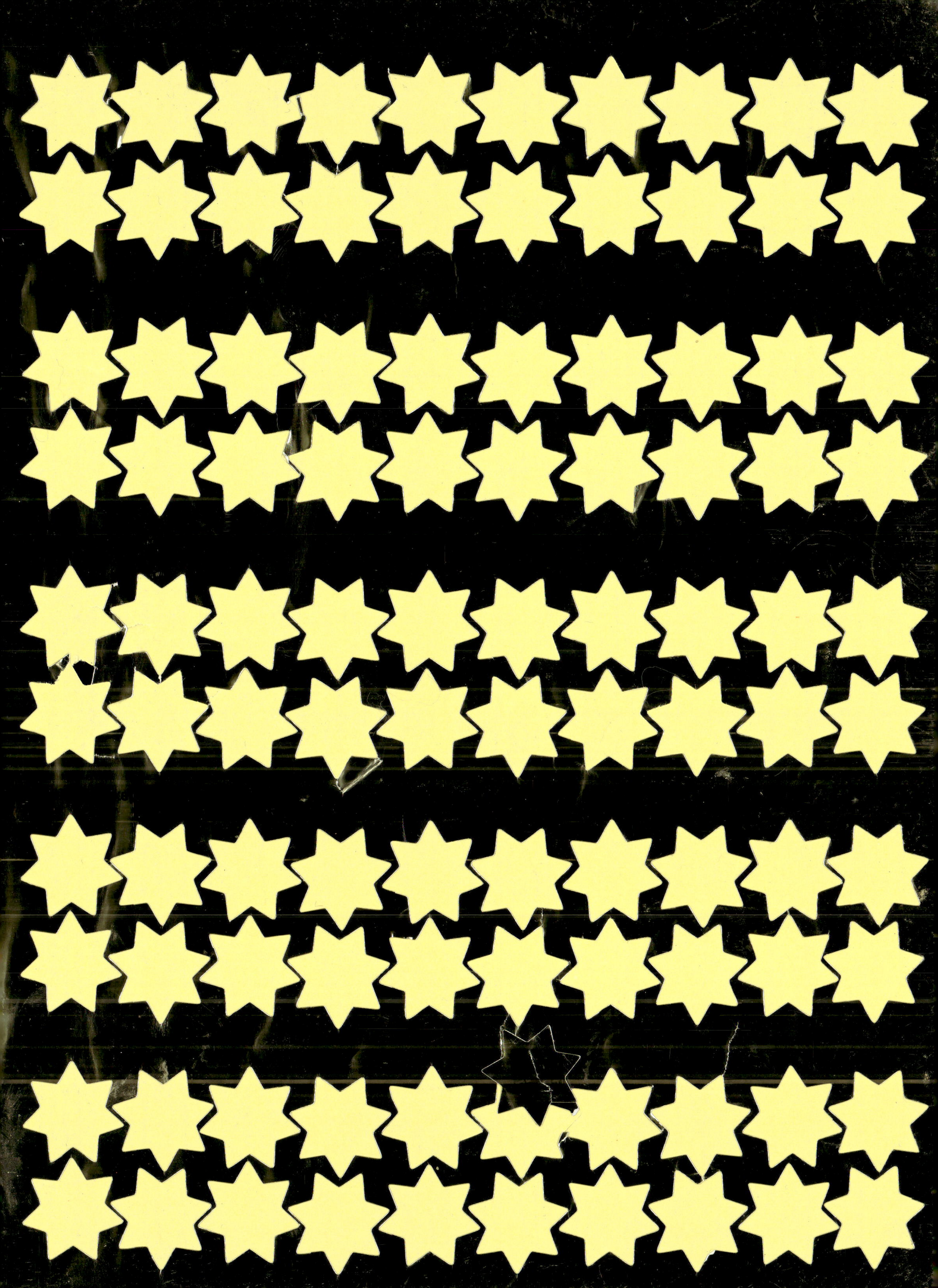

MY
TOP
100
ANIMALS

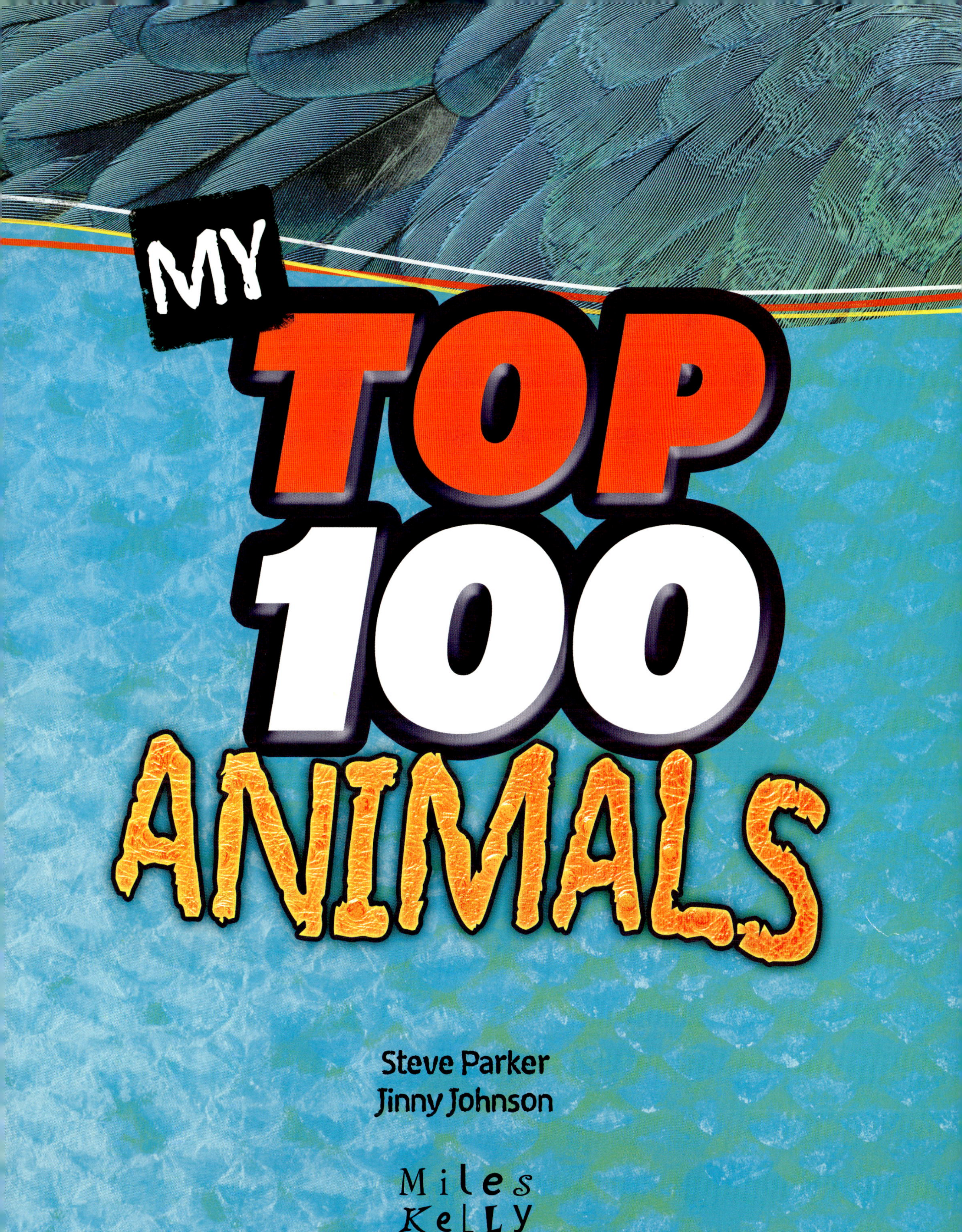
MY
TOP
100
ANIMALS
Steve Parker
Jinny Johnson
Miles
Kelly

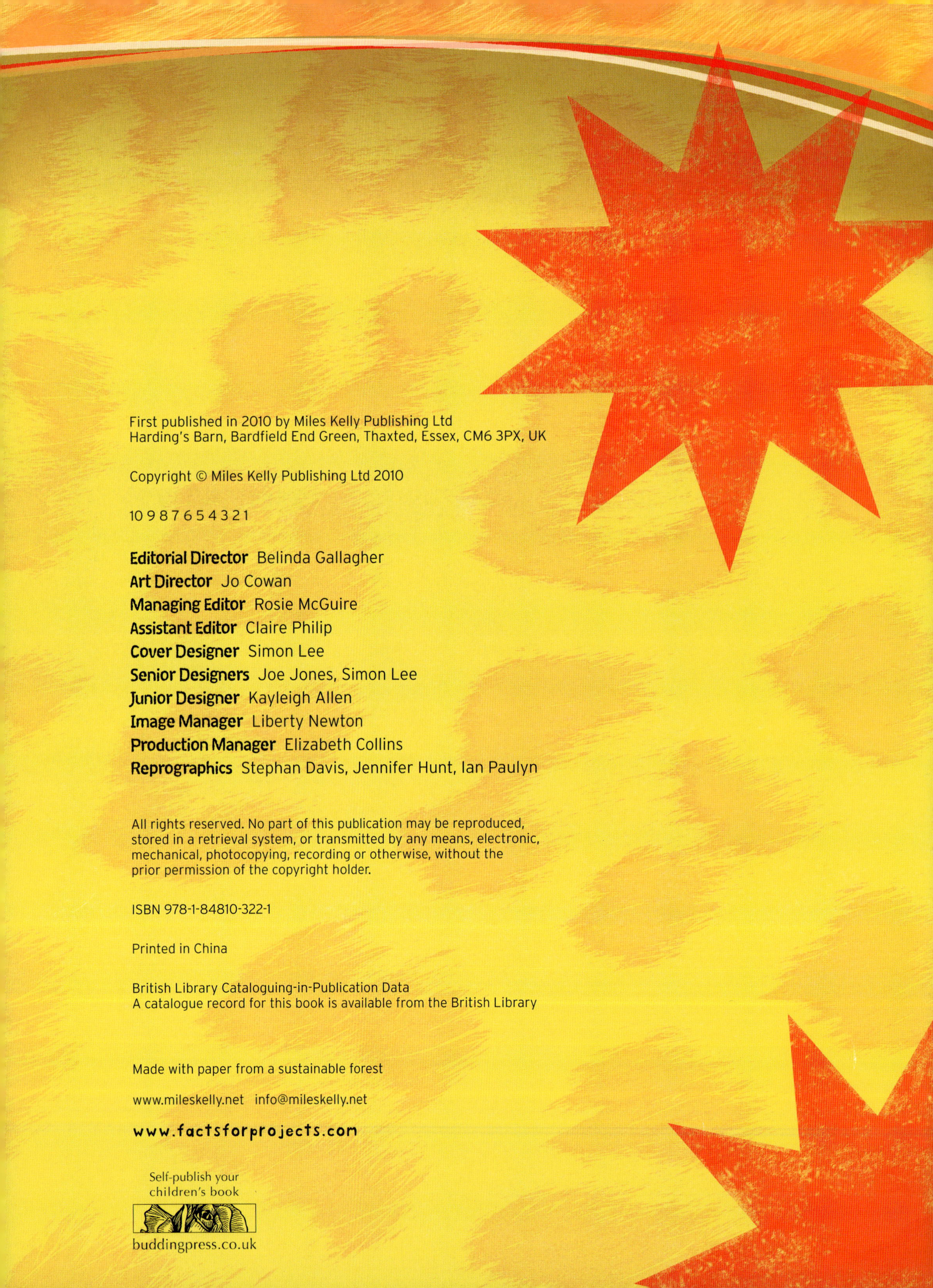

First published in 2010 by Miles Kelly Publishing Ltd
Harding's Barn, Bardfield End Green, Thaxted, Essex, CM6 3PX, UK

10 9 8 7 6 5 4 3 2 1

Editorial Director Belinda Gallagher
Art Director Jo Cowan
Managing Editor Rosie McGuire
Assistant Editor Claire Philip
Cover Designer Simon Lee
Senior Designers Joe Jones, Simon Lee
Junior Designer Kayleigh Allen
Image Manager Liberty Newton
Production Manager Elizabeth Collins
Reprographics Stephan Davis, Jennifer Hunt, Ian Paulyn

ISBN 978-1-84810-322-1

Printed in China

British Library Cataloguing-in-Publication Data
A catalogue record for this book is available from the British Library

Made with paper from a sustainable forest

www.mileskelly.net info@mileskelly.net

www.factsforprojects.com

CONTENTS

PREDATORS

EXTREME ANIMALS

WEIRD ANIMALS

ANIMAL GIANTS

SHARKS

HOW TO USE

This book is full of sensational facts about 100 amazing animals, divided into five cool sections. You can use the star stickers and cards provided to rate the animals in each section. Which animal is your favourite? **YOU DECIDE!**

STATUS

Every year the IUCN (the International Union for Conservation of Nature) produces a 'Red List' of threatened species. The conservation status of every animal and plant on the list is given a description.

Least Concern
The species is widespread and is not at risk.

Near Threatened
The species could be in trouble soon.

Vulnerable
The species is already under threat, and help is needed.

Endangered
The species faces big problems and the risk of extinction (dying out completely, forever) over the coming years is high.

Critically Endangered
The most serious group. Unless there is a huge conservation effort, extinction is just around the corner.

STAR RATING STICKERS

All the animals in this book are brilliant – but which ones are the best? Once you have read all the facts you can rate the animals in each section from one (your favourite) to 20 by placing the star stickers on the pages.

STAR CARDS

Each of the 100 animals featured in this book has its own rating card. Ask an adult to help you cut them all out.

The cards give you fast facts on each animal, divided into four categories. Each category is given a rating out of 20, with 20 being the highest score.

You can use your cards to learn vital statistics, or compare animals on their scores to help you decide which one is your favourite in each section.

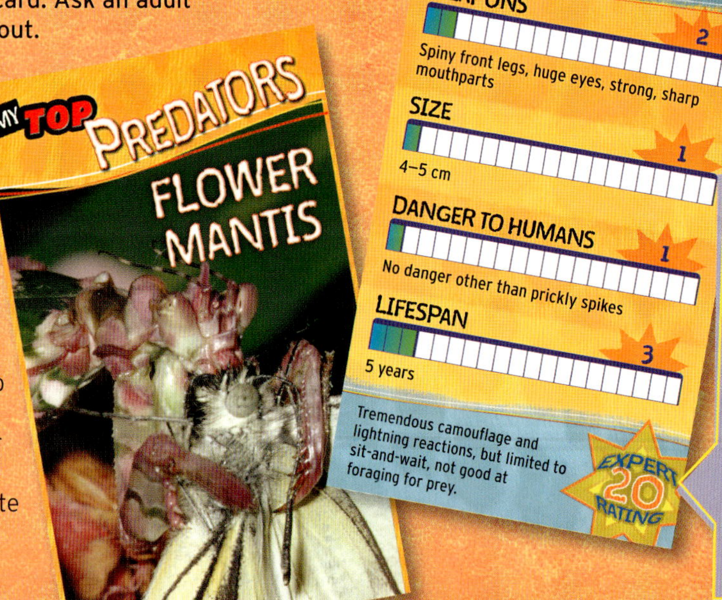

EXPERT RATING

Our authors have reviewed all the animals and given their verdict at the bottom of each card. The expert rating score shows where they think each of the animals stand in their section. Do you agree with their conclusions?

PREDATORS

IN FOR THE KILL

Being a hunter might seem an easy life. After a big meal of meaty nourishment, many predators laze around for days, or even weeks. Few other creatures threaten them, because they're so fierce and dangerous.

But that's only part of the story. When prey is scarce, a predator might weaken and starve through lack of food. After much time and effort tracking a target, the quarry (prey) could race off or slip away at any moment.

When it's finally time to go in for the kill, the victim will almost certainly fight back desperately. Predators need all their strength, speed, skills and weaponry to avoid injury and secure their feast.

As caribou migrate back into the snowy pine forests for winter, hungry wolves snap at their hooves. The pack members watch and wait for an old, young or sick individual to get slightly detached from the herd – and then its fate is sealed. If it attempts to flee, the pack gives chase. Closing in, the wolves race forwards from different directions to bite and then withdraw. The bewildered victim weakens from blood loss, and rapidly the wolves start their long-awaited feast.

'STAR' FACT

When food is very scarce, wolf packs may combine to increase hunting success rather than fight over scraps. One group observed in Alaska numbered more than 40!

PACK POWER

SNARL...

The pack leaders, or alpha pair, take the lion's share of a big kill. They make sure that lesser members know their place.

SPECIAL FEATURES

SCENT: The wolf's exceptionally keen nose picks up and follows scents that could be two or even three days old.

STAMINA: At a steady 'dogtrot', a wolf on the trail of prey can keep going for eight hours, gradually wearing down even the fleetest quarry.

Grey wolf

Scientific name: *Canis lupus*
Type: Mammal
Lifespan: 8–12 years
Length: Nose to tail-tip 2 m
Weight: 50-plus kg
Range: All northern lands
Status: Least concern

At a moderate pace, a wolf pack can eat up the miles when in pursuit of worthwhile big prey such as deer, wild sheep and goats.

HEARING: Like radar dishes, the wolf's ears swivel around to listen for faint sounds, not only from prey, but also from pack members and neighbouring packs.

COOPERATION: Two or three wolves may work together to ambush the biggest victims, such as an elk (moose) or bison ('buffalo').

Wild-eyed with terror, the victim struggles to escape the rock python's long fangs, stabbed in with devastating speed during its lightning strike. But the snake's muscular coils have begun to sneak around its body, settling into position as they tense like steel cables. With each of the prey's desperate breaths the coils tighten almost unnoticeably, so that the next breath becomes less possible. As air is squeezed away, so is life, and the python begins its long swallow.

DEATH HUG

SQUEEEZE...

A Thomson's gazelle loses its struggle as the rock python increases its grip. The gazelle will suffocate – or perhaps die of a heart attack.

SPECIAL FEATURES

CAMOUFLAGE: Dull greens and browns are ideal for hiding this massive snake among scrubby plants, rocks, soil, undergrowth – even in trees!

HEAT-SENSING PITS: Small hollows or pits, one under each eye, detect heat (infra-red rays) coming from warm-blooded prey.

Rock python

Scientific name: *Python sebae*
Type: Reptile
Lifespan: 25-plus years
Length: 6 m, exceptionally more
Weight: 70-plus kg
Range: Africa south of the Sahara
Status: Not enough information

STAR FACT

Several humans have become snacks for rock pythons over the years, usually young children. In 2009 a farmer was attacked by a rock python but used his mobile phone to summon help, and escaped.

GULP...

The python checks each meal's size and shape before working its extending mouth over one end. For the ground squirrel it's head-first, so that the legs slide in neatly.

MY STAR RATING

MUSCLES: Along the snake's length different blocks of the main body muscles squeeze or compress at different times to keep up overall relentless pressure.

JAWS: With several bones that make up the jaws being loosely connected, and slack jaw joints, the python's mouth can envelop prey wider than its head.

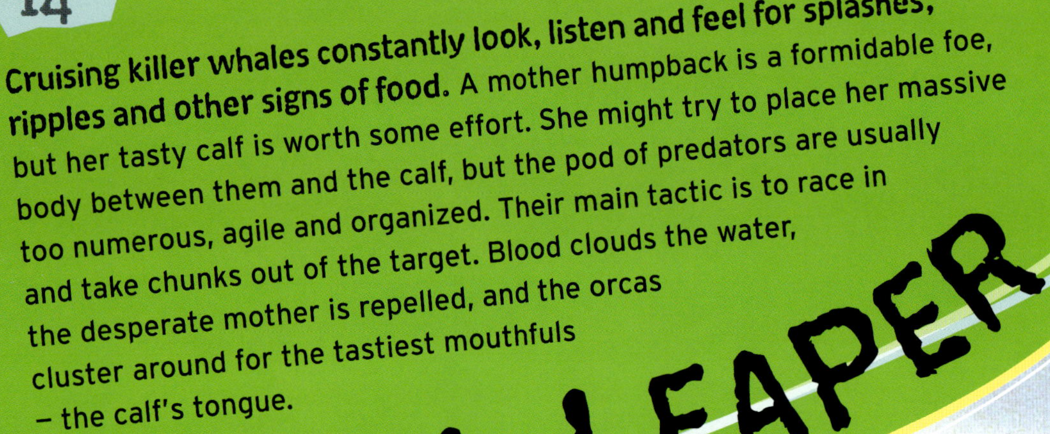

Cruising killer whales constantly look, listen and feel for splashes, ripples and other signs of food. A mother humpback is a formidable foe, but her tasty calf is worth some effort. She might try to place her massive body between them and the calf, but the pod of predators are usually too numerous, agile and organized. Their main tactic is to race in and take chunks out of the target. Blood clouds the water, the desperate mother is repelled, and the orcas cluster around for the tastiest mouthfuls – the calf's tongue.

LETHAL LEAPER

GOTCHA...

A killer whale rides on (and hides within) a breaking wave that takes it onto the beach to within a jaw-snap of a sea lion.

SPECIAL FEATURES

SPEED: A killer whale's super-streamlined body and great strength allows it to cut through open ocean at speeds of more than 60 km/h.

AGILITY: Able to turn completely around almost within its own length, the killer whale can also stay mobile underwater for more than 15 minutes.

SPLASH...

Killer whales are among the fastest animals in the sea, so breaching – leaping clear of the water and crashing back in – is easy. Breaching may be a form of communication between pod members.

Killer whale

Scientific name: *Orcinus orca*
Type: Mammal
Lifespan: Up to 60 years, rarely 80-plus
Length: Male up to 9 m, female 8 m
Weight: Male up to 6 tonnes, female 4 tonnes
Range: All seas and oceans
Status: Not enough information

STAR FACT

Killer whales have huge appetites, eating more than 220 kg of food daily – equivalent to the weight of four average adult humans.

COMMUNICATION: Pod members make varied squeaks and clicks that probably tell each other about food sources or threats such as big sharks.

INTELLIGENCE: Apart from learning many tasks in captivity, wild killer whales regularly devise new ways to hunt prey, such as trapping fish in shallow bays.

A tiger creeps through the long gloomy grass and scrub. It could be dusk, then again, it could be dawn. Tigers prefer to hunt in half-light, but if food is scarce, they will even bear the glare of the midday Sun. Tactics depend on the quarry. Generally it's a slow, sneaky stalk to within 50 metres of the target, then a massive charge as the big cat bursts from cover, leaps on the prey, and clamps its jaws and teeth onto the victim's neck to choke it to death.

STEALTH BITER

KEEP OUT...

Each tiger patrols and defends its own hunting area (territory), and marks it with droppings, urine and scratched trees. It must ensure enough prey for its own survival and so chases away rival and neighbouring tigers – except those of the opposite sex at breeding time.

SPECIAL FEATURES

APPETITE: A large adult tiger can eat almost 30 kg of food in one session, enough to sustain it for a week or more, but it needs water daily.

SIGHT: Cats' eyes are famously sensitive in the dark. A tiger can see objects more than 100 m away when humans can hardly peer 5 m.

Tiger

Scientific name: *Panthera tigris*
Type: Mammal
Lifespan: 10–20 years
Length: Head-body up to 2.5 m, tail up to 1 m
Weight: Up to 400 kg
Range: South, East and Southeast Asia
Status: Endangered/Critical

WATCH IT...

A fierce snarl warns others: 'Stay away from my prey!' Like all cats, except lions and cheetahs, tigers are solitary predators.

STAR FACT

Each tiger's stripes are as unique as our fingerprints, so human observers can identify individuals. The colouring is also in the skin – shave off a tiger's fur and it would still be striped!

MY STAR RATING

TEETH: The biggest teeth of any carnivore, the tiger's long canines stab and rip flesh. The rows of short incisors between them nibble the flesh from the bone.

SMELL: Tigers find prey such as deer, wild pigs and young buffalo by following scent trails. They also sniff out smaller animals such as lizards and even go fishing.

DEATHLY WINGS

The woods are quiet as night falls and a young barn owl takes off to hunt mice and voles. Without warning, powerful talons thud into its left side. The hunter becomes the hunted as the great eagle owl, flying noiselessly due to its soft-edged feathers, carries out its mid-air attack. The eagle owl has been scanning with its huge eyes and listening carefully for potential meals – just like the barn owl. Now the latter is mortally wounded and forced to the ground, where its huge relative begins a midnight supper.

GLIDE...

Small rodents such as rats, voles, lemmings and mice form the owl's main diet, but a young fox is also welcome.

SPECIAL FEATURES

SIGHT: Most owls can see much the same detail as humans, or better, but in light levels down to 100 times lower, which to us would be pitch black.

SOUND RECEPTION: The owl's 'facial disc' of feathers may help to gather sounds, like a radar bowl, and funnel them around to the ears.

LOOK OUT...

An owl's eyes occupy half of its head. Too large to swivel in their sockets, the bird must twist its neck instead – even to look behind itself.

STAR FACT

What look like tufted 'horns' or 'ears' are actually extra-long feathers on top of the eagle owl's head. The real ears are under the feathers on the sides of the head.

Eagle owl

Scientific name: *Bubo bubo*
Type: Bird
Lifespan: 15–20 years
Length: 75 cm
Wingspan: 2 m
Weight: Male 3 kg, female up to 4 kg
Range: Central Europe across to East Asia
Status: Least concern

HEARING: The eagle owl can locate prey by hearing alone using its amazingly sensitive ears, one offset slightly higher than the other on the head.

TERRITORY DEFENCE: Intruding owls that threaten an eagle owl's territory, which averages 40–50 sq km, are flapped at, pecked and scratched.

In deep water, where prey is scarce, it makes sense to ensure your catching technique is as secure as possible. The barracuda's long, fang-like teeth pierce a slippery victim deeply, so that it cannot wriggle and escape. Then with a massive gulp the meal is swallowed into the cavernous gullet. The whole event lasts just three seconds, and the sleek, speedy predator may not eat again for three weeks.

FATAL FANGS

Barracuda

Scientific name: *Sphyraena* (various species)
Type: Fish
Lifespan: 10–15 years
Length: Up to 1.8 m
Weight: Up to 50 kg
Range: Warmer seas and oceans
Status: Not assessed

BACK OFF...

On the edge of the twilight zone, 500 m below the ocean surface, a deep-sea barracuda emerges from the shadows and bares its fangs to ward off threats.

STAR FACT

Great barracudas are known to attack human divers, nipping them hard to see if they are tasty enough for a full attack.

MY STAR RATING

SPECIAL FEATURES

SPEED: Barracudas are long, slim and big-tailed, designed for fast acceleration as they burst into action and grab prey with a lightning dash.

SIGHT: The eyes are especially large in deep-water barracuda species, allowing them to see the shadowy shapes of prey in the gloom.

RAZOR TEETH

Piranhas can be peaceful, feeding as quiet individuals on worms, water bugs and even fallen fruits. But the slightest scent of blood or body fluids makes a shoal mass together to search for the source. Within seconds of finding it they hurl themselves into a feeding frenzy as they snap and slice with their blade-like teeth. They can become so frantic that they even take chunks out of each other.

Red-bellied piranha

Scientific name: *Pygocentrus nattereri*
Type: Fish
Lifespan: 10 years
Length: 30–40 cm
Weight: 3 kg
Range: Central America, North to Central South America
Status: Least concern

SLASH...

The thin, triangular teeth easily cut into skin and tough flesh. The fish clamps its jaws and shakes from side to side to rip off a morsel.

STAR FACT

Stories about piranha shoals stripping all flesh from a large animal such as a cow, leaving only the skeleton, are – true!

MY STAR RATING

SPECIAL FEATURES

SENSES: A stripe along each side of the body, the lateral line, detects ripples so that the piranha can find a struggling animal even in the dark.

SPEED: Using their lateral lines, feeding piranhas sense where other shoal members are, dash in, take a bite and withdraw, all in half a second.

Nile crocodiles wait patiently as thundering hooves, snorts and swirling dust announce that the annual wildebeest trek has reached the river once more. Tumbling and plunging into the water, the 'beests set off in panic to the other side. But hidden menaces approach those swimming along the edge of the main group. Suddenly one wildebeest roars in pain, thrashes wildly – and disappears. A crocodile drags it under until it drowns, then prepares to 'death-roll' and rip a haunch from the corpse.

ON A ROLL

STAR FACT

In the 'death roll' the croc grabs part of the prey animal's body and then spins like a top to twist and tear a lump of flesh away from the main carcass.

FULL UP...

After an enormous meal the Nile crocodile may not need to eat again for four months or more.

SPECIAL FEATURES

SPEED: With a swish of its mighty tail, a croc can accelerate to cover three times its body length in hardly a second.

TEETH: Ongoing replacement and growth happen when a tooth wears and falls out or is damaged. Teeth of different ages give the 'ragged smile' look.

OUCH...

Once the jaws clamp onto a victim with a crunching clench, the battle is almost over. The croc can hang on for hours; the wildebeest cannot.

Nile crocodile

Scientific name: *Crocodylus niloticus*
Type: Reptile
Lifespan: 50-plus years
Length: Male up to 5.5 m, female 4 m
Weight: Male up to 570 kg, female 300 kg
Range: North-east, Central and Southern Africa
Status: Least concern

MY STAR RATING

BITE POWER: The croc's jaw strength and bite pressure have been measured as exceeding those of a great white shark and a lion.

DEFENCE: Crocodile skin is thick and leathery, covered by very hard scales and contains plates of bone within its thickness, for three-layered protection.

With its curiously cramped, crab-like gait, the huntsman spider stalks along a branch in search of a suitable snack. Perhaps a beetle or small lizard, a resting cricket or sleepy moth – even a baby bird in its nest. When the spider detects vibrations that indicate a nearby animal, it swivels around to give its beady eyes a good view. Creeping stealthily into range, it suddenly lunges, grabs with its forelegs, and jabs in venom with its fearsome fangs.

CREEPY POISONER

STAR FACT

Huntsman spiders are also called rain spiders because they seek shelter from storms by hiding in garages, sheds and houses. If you found one in your house, how would you react?

ATTACK...

With its two venomous fangs partly hidden by long hairs, the huntsman is poised to attack, and can subdue a lizard bigger than itself.

SPECIAL FEATURES

SPEED: Huntsman spiders are also called giant crab spiders. Their long, curved, forward-arching legs equip them for sudden sprints.

TOUCH: Hairs on the huntsman's legs are very sensitive to air movements, while its feet detect vibrations caused by animals moving nearby.

Huntsman spider

Scientific name: *Heteropoda, Palystes* and others
Type: Arachnid
Lifespan: 15-plus years
Legspan: Up to 30 cm
Range: Tropical areas including Southeast Asia, Australia, Southern Africa
Status: Not assessed

Like other arachnids, insects and crabs, a huntsman grows by shedding its old skin (exoskeleton). The soft new one beneath expands before it hardens.

VISION: Huntsman spiders do not build webs. Instead their eight main forward-facing eyes give excellent vision for tracking and tackling prey.

POISON: Huntsman venom paralyzes its small victims in seconds. It can cause swelling, nausea and headaches in humans, but death is exceptionally rare.

The largest land-based carnivore, the polar bear's main food is seals, particularly bearded seals and ringed seals. A polar bear may shuffle quietly across ice towards a resting seal, then dash the last few metres before the seal can wriggle into the water to escape. Or it will wait patiently by a breathing hole, perhaps for several hours, for a seal to pop its head out. Then suddenly the bear pounces, using its enormous forepaws to hook the seal out onto the ice before delivering a massive, skull-cracking bite.

ARCTIC ASSASSIN

COOL...

Younger polar bears play-fight to practise their killing manoeuvres and develop powerful muscles.

SPECIAL FEATURES

FUR: The long hairs of the outer 'guard' layer of a polar bear's coat may be more than 10 cm in length. They are not white but transparent.

BLUBBER: Under the bear's skin is a fatty layer of insulating blubber. At the coldest times of year, when prey is scarce, it may be over 10 cm thick.

YUMMY...

A 50-kg seal will be mostly devoured, especially the rich blubber under its skin, which provides the bear with energy, helping it stay warm.

Polar bear

Scientific name: *Ursus maritimus*
Type: Mammal
Lifespan: 20 years
Length: Male up to 3 m, female 2.5 m
Weight: Male up to 600 kg, female 300 kg
Range: Far northern lands and seas
Status: Vulnerable

STAR FACT

When lack of sea ice prevents polar bears from catching their usual meaty prey, they may resort to berries, plant buds and even seaweed!

MY STAR RATING

PAWS: The enormous paws, up to 30 cm wide, work as weight-distributing snowshoes on land and as paddles when swimming. The furry soles grip ice well.

SMELL: With the wind in the right direction, and few other scents to interfere, a polar bear can detect a whale or seal carcass from 5 km or more away.

The golden eagle can soar on high, spotting prey as small as voles from more than one kilometre away. Or it may drift low behind trees and suddenly carry out a surprise attack, spearing its talons into a victim such as a rabbit. The eagle's flapping muscles and vast wings have enough power to lift loads that few other flyers could manage. Usually the eagle carries its prize to its eyrie (nest) and tears it apart for its own consumption – or for its offspring.

WINGED BUTCHER

GROSS...

The eagle makes short work of victims by holding them down with its talons and tearing off lumps of the juiciest flesh like an expert butcher, using its sharp-edged, hook-tipped bill.

SPECIAL FEATURES

SIGHT: Large eyes adapted for long-distance vision mean a golden eagle can see details almost ten times farther away than humans can.

FLIGHT: Soaring on updraughts of air among the mountains allows the eagle to circle for hours without a flap, saving energy for that killer swoop.

Golden eagle

Scientific name: *Aquila chrysaetos*
Type: Bird
Lifespan: 30-plus years
Length: 1 m
Wingspan: 2.4 m
Weight: 6 kg
Range: Temperate northern lands
Status: Least concern

STAR FACT

In many areas, rabbits and hares form more than half of the eagle's diet. Larger prey include deer fawns, the young of wild sheep and goats, and in one case, even a bear cub.

SWOOP...

With wing and tail flight feathers fanned to slow its speed, a golden eagle's outstretched talons are ready to impale a meal in their iron grip.

MY STAR RATING

TALONS: Each foot claw is curved almost at a right angle, and on contact the front and rear toes swing together, nearly meeting inside the victim's body.

STRENGTH: It's estimated that a golden eagle can fly while carrying a load of half its own body weight. Larger victims are ripped apart where they died.

Like its cousins, the true spiders, a solifuge or sun-spider is a terrifically efficient eight-legged hunting machine. Also known as the camel spider, sun-scorpion or wind-scorpion, the solifuge can stalk slowly or sprint with breathtaking speed. Most likely to dash out from a shady crack under a rock and sink its fangs into prey, its food varies from small beetles and worms up to lizards and birds bigger than itself.

SHADY STALKER

STAR FACT

'Solifuge' means 'sun-hider'. Local people have long checked their clothes and footwear before getting dressed, in case a solifuge has sought shade inside.

SPECIAL FEATURES

SIGHT: The solifuge has small eyes on the front part of its main body, which sense little detail but register movement very accurately.

FANGS: The two 'fangs' (chelicerae) are hinged to work like pointed, stabbing pincers, and they are moved by extremely powerful muscles.

Solifuge

Scientific name: *Eremorhax* and others
Type: Arachnid
Lifespan: 10-plus years
Length: Body up to 10 cm
Legspan: Up to 15 cm
Range: Much of North America, Africa, Asia
Status: Not assessed

PALPS: Two long sensory parts called palps, one on either side of the head just in front of the first true leg, pick up vibrations and help to restrain prey.

LEGS: The first pair of true legs are shorter and specialized for holding victims, while the other six legs are long for exceptionally rapid running.

Almost any creature that can be stuffed into its wide mouth is fair game for the horned frog – even other horned frogs. Mice, lizards, fish, and large insects and worms are also consumed into the sticky, sharp-edged, tough-skinned, gulping jaws. After a full feast this frog – which usually appears to consist of just a mouth, eyes, stomach and four little limbs – looks even more plump and rotund than normal.

BIG MOUTH

Horned frog

Scientific name: *Ceratophrys cornuta*
Type: Amphibian
Lifespan: 4–6 years
Length: Male 18 cm, female 22 cm
Weight: Up to 1 kg
Range: Northern South America
Status: Least concern

SLURP...

The horned frog may not look speedy, but its sudden lunge from under leaves or within undergrowth is a deadly surprise for most prey.

STAR FACT

Even though its mouth is as wide as its whole head, sometimes a victim is too big and the horned frog may choke to death.

SPECIAL FEATURES

DEFENCE: The leathery skin is difficult for predators to grasp, and the frog also oozes foul liquid, hisses and kicks out in self defence.

TEETH: Unusually among frogs and toads, the horned frog has small teeth in its upper jaw, which help to subdue kicking, thrashing prey.

SUDDEN STRIKE

Coiled around a branch, the eyelash viper can remain perfectly still for hours. The onset of night brings the best feeding time as the snake use its eyes and the heat-sensitive pit organs just beneath them to assess its surroundings in total darkness. If a mouse or tree-rat wanders within range, the snake strikes with lightning speed, delivers its paralyzing venom and begins its meal.

STRIKE...

Poison, quickly injected through the viper's fangs, affects the victim's blood, brain and nerve system.

Eyelash viper

Scientific name: *Bothriechis schlegelii*
Type: Reptile
Lifespan: 8–12 years
Length: 80 cm
Weight: 2 kg
Range: Forests of Central and South America
Status: Not assessed

'STAR FACT

The 'eyelashes' of this viper are actually angled scales that help with camouflage by breaking up the recognizable outline of the head.

SPECIAL FEATURES

PITS: Small hollows, one between each eye and nostril, detect the heat or infra-red rays from warm-blooded prey even in darkness.

FOLDING FANGS: The two long upper front teeth, normally pointing rearwards, fold or tilt down to jab venom into the prey.

BONE CRUNCHERS

Hyaenas are famed as scavengers, but they are also efficient teamwork hunters in their own right. A large group or clan, perhaps 30-plus strong, can harass and bring down game as big as a young giraffe. Or, if the opportunity arises, they can force a small pride of lions away from their kill by snarling, baring their massively strong teeth and jaws, and continually darting at the big cats to taunt and snap. Once the lions have gone, the hyaenas munch and crunch. Even hide (skin) and bones are greedily gulped down.

The 'laughing' hyaena's giggling yelp usually tells other clan members: 'Back off, this is my food!'

SPECIAL FEATURES

JAWS: Massive jaw bones and chewing muscles allow hyaenas to crack open bones to get at the nutritious marrow inside.

TEETH: A hyaena's teeth are larger than average for its body size, especially the bone-crushing premolars and shearing molars (at front and back).

Spotted hyaena

Scientific name: *Crocuta crocuta*
Type: Mammal
Lifespan: 10–12 years
Length: Male 1.6 m, female up to 1.8 m
Weight: Male 65 kg, female up to 70 kg
Range: Central, East and Southern Africa
Status: Least concern

CHOMP...

There's no time for manners as the hyaenas plunge into the carcass innards, consuming first the flesh and guts, then sinew and bone.

STAR FACT

Behaviour and body language indicates an individual's rank in the clan. 'Crawling' (keeping low to the ground when moving) is a low-ranking hyaena's way of showing submission to the boss.

MY STAR RATING

DIGESTION: Extra-strong digestive acids and juices make short work of swallowed bony bits, dissolving them to extract as much goodness as possible.

STRENGTH: Hyaenas' powerful shoulders and front legs, used for tearing prey and self-defence, contrast with their sloping backs and smaller rumps and rear legs.

Penguins beware! The leopard seal sometimes strikes from below, rising from the deep with the tiniest swish to sink its teeth into the bird's chest fat and flesh. Or this long, slim, sneaky speedster may lie in wait under the edge of an iceberg, then dash out as a penguin dives in, so fast that the unlucky victim plunges head-first into its jaws. When penguins are too scared to swim, the leopard seal switches to fish, squid, or perhaps a smaller seal such as the crabeater.

SNEAK ATTACK

Terrified penguins huddle on a mound in the centre of an ice floe as a leopard seal patrols the surrounding waters.

BEWARE...

Leopard seal

Scientific name: *Hydrurga leptonyx*
Type: Mammal
Lifespan: 22–28 years
Length: Male 3.4 m, female up to 3.8 m
Weight: Male 400 kg, female up to 500 kg
Range: Southern Ocean, Antarctica
Status: Least concern

SWIMMING: Cruising with hardly a ripple, the seal accelerates to full speed in a split second, and twists and turns after the most agile prey.

BREATHING: Holding its breath for more than 30 minutes means the leopard seal can surprise penguins that thought it was long gone.

STAR FACT

The first recorded human death from a leopard seal happened in 2003, when a snorkelling research scientist was dragged under and drowned.

YIKES...

If a swimming penguin gets this close to a leopard seal, it's staring death in the face. With only one-tenth of a second to react, it's probably already too late.

SENSES AND STRENGTH: This seal can see a resting penguin or seal through thin ice from below, swim up and smash through, right in front of the victim.

TEETH: The 3-cm-long, dog-like canine teeth are ideal to jab into the prey as the seal shakes the life out of it and rips it into smaller chunks that it can swallow.

A butterfly flutters down to sip nectar from a beautiful flower, unaware that among the petals sits death in disguise – a spiny **flower mantis.** Its eyes swivel to check the butterfly's distance, then in a flash, the jack-knife front legs shoot fowards and snap together to impale the victim with their strong spines. The mantis settles down to chew off the butterfly's head, then nibbles its way along the body. Eating the wings too means it's really hungry.

STAR FACT

This insect's bent front limbs give it the common name 'praying' mantis, as though its hands are together in worship – but it is far more efficient at 'preying'.

FATAL PETAL

TRAPPED...

The jointed front legs work like spiked scissors that flick shut powerfully and instantly.

SPECIAL FEATURES

SIGHT: The huge eyes of the mantis are almost as large as the rest of the head and see not only great detail but also very fast movements.

FORELEGS: The fierce thorn-like spines on the front legs stab deep into prey so that it cannot struggle free.

Flower mantis

Scientific name: *Pseudocreobotra* and others (various species)
Type: Insect
Lifespan: 5 years
Length: 4–5 cm
Wingspan: 6 cm
Range: East and Southern Africa
Status: Not assessed

Keeping very still while on view is key to the mantis' hunting success. 'Petals' that move will scare away visitors at once.

CAMOUFLAGE: Each flower mantis has a unique pattern of colours and shapes, mainly pinks and greens, and selects a flower of the same hues in which to lurk.

MOUTHPARTS: The mantis has two sharp-edged mandibles that move sideways (not up and down), coming together in the centre like powerful pincers.

Dogged pursuit is the speciality of African wild dogs. Once a pack latches onto the scent of an antelope or similar quarry, they can run for hours... and hours... The prey is finally exhausted and panting when the dogs rush in for a massed attack. Snapping and scratching, the pack's lead hunters grab the animal's nose and rear unprotected underbelly. Within seconds, the dogs start to gorge their fill. Within a minute, death is merciful.

TEAM SLAYERS

STAR FACT

The African wild dog is a champion eater. It can gulp down more than 10 kg – about one-third of its own weight – of muscle, sinew, chewed skin and crushed bone.

NO ESCAPE...

Even if the wind blows the scent of prey animals away from the wild dog's ultra-sensitive nose, its rounded ears will pick up distant munching sounds, hoof-falls and snorts.

SPECIAL FEATURES

APPETITE: The wild dogs' legendary stomach capacity means they consume a carcass before hungry lions or scavenging hyaenas muscle in.

STAMINA: With their long legs and lean build, wild dogs are relatively lightweight but still well muscled. They easily trot 20 km during a hunt.

African wild dog

Scientific name: *Lycaon pictus*
Type: Mammal
Lifespan: 12–18 years
Shoulder height: 75 cm
Length: Head-body 90 cm, tail 35 cm
Weight: 25–30 kg
Range: East and Southern Africa
Status: Endangered

DOOMED...

A wildebeest struggles in vain under the combined teeth and pulling power of a wild dog pack. A dozen or more dogs cluster around, subdue the animal and start to feed.

COMMUNICATION: Pack individuals keep in contact with strange, bird-like cheeps, twitters and mini-yelps to coordinate the hunt's progress and tactics.

TEAMWORK: 'Outrider' and 'pursuer' dogs guide the victim towards the bigger, stronger members that lead the final assault.

High diver and expert marine predator, the gannet makes spectacular plunges into the sea from as much as 40 metres above the surface. It dive-bombs into the waves at high speed, seizes a fish or squid with its long dagger-like beak and quickly gulps it down as it surfaces again. Gannets are also strong long-distance fliers, soaring for miles over the sea as they search for prey.

DIVE BOMBER

HERE I COME!

A gannet's diving skills make it a far more efficient predator than the seagulls flapping over the surface of the ocean.

SPECIAL FEATURES

WEBBED FEET: Strong webbed feet make the gannet a fast, powerful swimmer. It also uses its feet as brakes when flying.

PROTECTED NOSTRILS: A small flap of bone protects the gannet's nostrils, preventing water from being forced into the nostrils during the bird's high-speed dives.

STAR FACT

A plunge-diving gannet hits the water at amazing speed – up to 100 km/h. Their speed at impact carries gannets deeper than most other diving birds so they can catch prey that others cannot reach.

Gannet

Scientific name: *Morus bassanus*
Type: Bird
Lifespan: 16–21 years
Length: 87–100 cm; wingspan 1.6–1.8 m
Weight: 2.4–3.6 kg
Range: North Atlantic, Mediterranean
Status: Least concern

GREEDY ...

When gannets find a shoal of fish there's a feeding frenzy. The birds dive down and swim around under the surface, gobbling up the fish.

MY STAR RATING

STRONG SKULL: Air-filled spaces, crossed by struts of bones, help to strengthen the gannet's skull and protect it when the bird hits the water.

STREAMLINING: As it enters the water, the gannet holds its wings swept back and its head and body straight so it cuts into the water like a torpedo.

TINY TERROR

Smallest of the mammal carnivores, the least weasel will tackle prey five times its own size. It attacks in a furious flurry of teeth, claws and blood, usually biting the back of the neck to damage the spinal cord nerve and paralyze the prey. It needs to eat often, gobbling up to half of its own body weight daily in winter to stay warm and fuel its darting, sniffing, leaping, action-packed hunting style.

Least weasel

Scientific name: *Mustela nivalis*
Type: Mammal
Lifespan: 5–6 years
Length: Male 23 cm, female 19 cm
Weight: Up to 50 g
Range: Most northern lands
Status: Least concern

STAR FACT

Its head is hardly larger than that of a mouse or vole, so the least weasel can easily pursue these prey into their burrows.

HEAVE...

This young rabbit should keep the weasel going for a couple of days. Any leftover bits of the carcass may then be stored in a den.

SPECIAL FEATURES

AGILITY: A leaping least weasel can turn around twice in mid air, so the confused prey does not know from which side the attack will come.

REACTIONS: Lightning responses allow the least weasel to dart underneath large prey and launch a neck bite from the opposite side.

EXTREME ANIMALS

PUSHING THE LIMITS

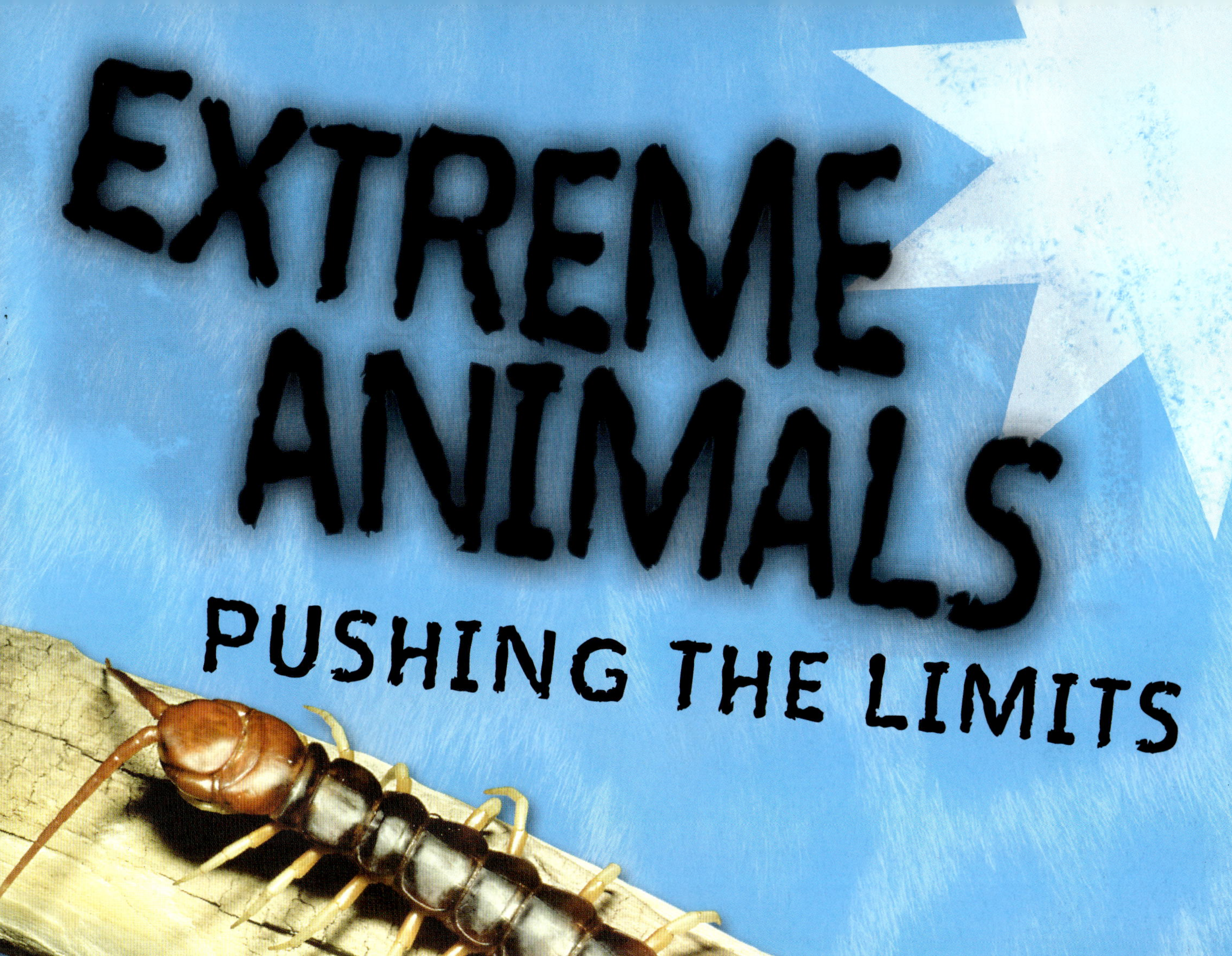

Out in the wild, danger lurks behind every tree, leaf, rock and ledge, and in any dark corner. The natural world is extremely perilous, so it pays to be extreme too. Being not just slightly better than the rest, but way out ahead, brings more chance of survival.

However, going to extremes does have its problems. Really massive creatures may be powerful, but they are also huge, slow targets for predators. Animals that have adapted to thrive in the harshest conditions might not cope if these conditions change. Like the rest of nature, it's a continual balancing act to be extreme, but not excessive.

Famed as the fastest fish in the sea, the sailfish is an open-ocean hunter of smaller shoaling fish such as mackerel and anchovies. Where these gather, so do loose groups of sailfish. They circle the prey at extreme speed, forcing them into a tight rounded bunch know as a baitball. If the prey start to scatter, the sailfish suddenly erect their folded fins to frighten them back into the ball. Then the sailfish dash at the ball to stun and gobble up the quarry.

SPRINTER SAILOR

NO WAY OUT...

Like wolves circling deer, sailfish drive their food into a compact clump, so greatly increasing the chances of capture.

SPECIAL FEATURES

TAIL: The caudal fin (tail) is slim, stiff and crescent-shaped – the perfect shape for speedy swimming with limited manoeuvrability.

SAIL DOWN: Usually the dorsal fin or sail, which is held up by long, bony fin rays (rods), is folded down along the top or upper side of the body.

Sailfish

Scientific name: *Istiophorus albicans* (Atlantic sailfish)
Type: Fish
Lifespan: 4–5 years
Length: 3 m
Weight: 60–70 kg
Range: Atlantic, Caribbean
Status: Not assessed

SWIPE...

The long, pointed snout is known as the bill. The sailfish uses its bill to jab at fish in the baitball as it swims past. Then it rushes back in to swallow them whole.

STAR FACT

Estimates for sailfish speed vary, but the upper limits are thought to be in the region of 100–110 km/h, which is about the same as the cheetah on land.

MY STAR RATING

SAIL UP: When the sailfish quickly extends its massive dorsal fin, smaller fish are scared into a panic, making them easier to target.

BILL: Apart from being a hunting weapon, the sword-like bill is also used in self defence against sharks and killer whales, and is excellent for streamlining.

As the world's tallest animal, the giraffe has several advantages over other African bush plant-eaters. It can reach leaves higher in trees, see farther for approaching danger, and lope along at a seemingly leisurely gallop that soon leaves other creatures far behind. But there are drawbacks too. Eating low plants and drinking mean awkward stooping and great effort. Mating is tricky and ungainly. And when a baby giraffe is born, it's in for quite a fall.

HIGHEST LIFE

GO LOW...

A giraffe must splay its front legs widely in order to bend its shoulders and neck enough to drink at the waterhole.

STAR FACT

The giraffe's neck is as long as a human adult is tall. Yet inside it are just seven neck bones – the same number as there are in the necks of humans and other mammals.

SPECIAL FEATURES

NECK: Apart from extra-high feeding, the heavy, muscular neck can be swung around like a battering ram to bash rivals or predators.

HOOVES: The giraffe can strike out surprisingly suddenly and reach a long way with its sharp-edged hooves, which are as wide as dinner plates.

Giraffe

Scientific name: *Giraffa camelopardalis*
Type: Mammal
Lifespan: 20–25 years
Height: Male 5.5 m, female 4.5 m
Weight: Male 1.4 tonnes, female 800 kg
Range: Mainly east and southern Africa
Status: Least concern

LOOK...

Everything about the giraffe is extremely elongated, including its face and nose, which give added reach when browsing tree-tops.

MY STAR RATING

MOUTH AND LIPS: Thick, tough skin around the lips and mouth mean that the giraffe is rarely bothered by prickly plants, even sharp-thorned acacia trees.

TONGUE: Extending the exceptionally long, flexible, grasping tongue adds another 50 cm to the giraffe's feeding height.

Supreme aerial hunter, the peregrine falcon preys mainly on fellow fliers. Its diet includes medium-sized birds from starlings to pigeons, plus the occasional bat, and ground-dwellers such as voles, rats, squirrels and young rabbits. Famed for its extreme speed when diving, the peregrine seemingly streaks down from nowhere to slam into its quarry with its sharp talons (claws), which then pierce and clasp the stunned victim.

AIR ACE KILLER

STAR FACT

The peregrine is the world's most widespread bird of prey. Despite its speed and agility in the air, it can fall victim to its larger cousins such as the golden eagle and eagle owl.

ON GUARD...

Peregrines nest on the ledges of cliffs and man-made structures such as bridges and skyscrapers. The mother guards the chicks at the nest as the male brings them food.

SPECIAL FEATURES

WINGS: The peregrine's wings are broad and back-swept, tapering to a point at the tip – the best design for speed and aerobatic manoeuvres.

TALONS: The powerful talons close on prey with a strong grip and hold it while the peregrine plucks and dismembers it.

Peregrine falcon

Scientific name: *Falco peregrinus*
Type: Bird
Lifespan: 15–20 years
Length: Male 45 cm, female 55 cm
Weight: Male 0.7 kg, female 1.2 kg
Range: Worldwide except polar regions, New Zealand
Status: Least concern

PREPARE TO DIVE...

As a peregrine enters its power-dive or 'stoop' to attack a lower-flying bird victim, it becomes the fastest of all animals, reaching speeds of more than 340 km/h.

MY STAR RATING

BILL: Typically hooked and sharp-tipped for ripping flesh, the bill also has a small notch in the upper part to cut or break the neck of its prey.

EYESIGHT: Huge eyes mean the high-flying peregrine can spot fast-moving prey from above, against the backdrop of the ground below.

In tip-top breeding condition, ready to dominate his patch of beach, the elephant seal can be one of nature's truly awesome sights. With his massive rearing bulk and fearsome, ear-splitting roars, he challenges other males who try to take over his batch of females. The name 'elephant' comes mainly from this seal's long, floppy nose, but it could be from his enormous size. In best seasonal condition a well-fed male can tip the scales at 4 tonnes, which is as heavy as a real elephant.

BEACH MASTER

STAR FACT

Elephant seals come ashore for between two and three months to breed, but they spend the rest of the year in the deep, cold ocean.

The vast dominant males, called alphas or 'beachmasters', defend their territories in vicious fights in which they push, clash and bite for hours.

FIGHT...

SPECIAL FEATURES

SIZE: The male's huge, heavyweight body helps when battling rival males at breeding time. Only the winners will mate with the females.

PROTECTION: A thick layer of blubber (fat) under the skin retains body warmth in cold seas and protects against the slashing teeth of rivals.

Elephant seal

Scientific name: *Mirounga leonina* (Southern elephant seal)
Type: Mammal
Lifespan: Male 20 years, female 25 years
Length: Male 6 m, female 3 m
Weight: Male up to 5 tonnes, female 650 kg
Range: Southern oceans, seas and islands
Status: Least concern

Other wildlife, such as king penguins, keep a safe distance as a male elephant seal prepares to take over a patch of beach.

DIVING: In extreme cases the elephant seal can hold its breath for two hours as it dives to depths of more than 1000 m to hunt for food.

FEEDING: Squid and fish are the main items on the elephant seal's menu, but it can also crunch up crabs, lobsters and shellfish such as clams.

Hmmm, bzzzz, mmmm ... a hummingbird's special humming sound comes from its wings, which in some species beat up to 100 times each second. This fast flapping allows the tiny bird to hover like a helicopter, and even fly sideways and backwards. But such an energy-intensive way of moving means that hummingbirds are constantly in need of food, chiefly sugary plant saps and flower nectar.

HURRIED HUMMER

A hovering hummingbird holds its main body vertical (upright) so that its wings push air almost straight downwards. Faster flapping means that it will rise straight upwards.

HOVER...

SPECIAL FEATURES

WINGS: The slim, triangular, pointed wings are excellent for speedy flaps, although the design is poor for gliding and soaring.

SIGHT: The hummingbird's colour vision is acute, allowing it to pick out suitable nectar-rich flowers as well as catch the occasional bug or spider.

Black-throated hummingbird

Scientific name: *Anthracothorax nigricollis* and others
Type: Bird
Lifespan: 5–7 years
Length: 10 cm
Weight: 7 g
Range: South America
Status: Least concern

STAR FACT

Some types of hummingbird make long migrations (seasonal journeys), covering distances of more than 3000 km. The human equivalent would be halfway to the Moon!

ME, ME...

Courting female (left) and male black-throated mango hummingbirds swoop, dive, hover and peck imaginary blooms, as each tries to impress the other.

BEAK: The extremely long, thin, slightly down-curved beak is the best shape for probing deeply into the middle of flowers.

TONGUE: The lengthy tongue laps nectar and also tastes its sugar content, so the bird does not waste time feeding at flowers where nectar is thin and diluted.

Probably the most poisonous fish in the sea, the stonefish could also win the title of the ugliest. But its tubby body, lumpy skin, strange fins and mottled colours are ideal camouflage among reefs and rocks in the shallows. Here this ambush predator waits, lying quite still, until a smaller fish, shrimp or similar creature swims by. Then with a sudden lunge the stonefish open its huge mouth and sucks in the meal.

DEADLY VENOM

Stonefish

Scientific name: Synanceia (several species)
Type: Fish
Lifespan: Not known, perhaps 10 years
Length: 40 cm
Range: Shallow tropical seas of Pacific and Indian Ocean
Status: Not enough information

People paddling in the shallows may not see a half-buried stonefish until they step on its poison spines and feel the first waves of stinging pain.

OUCH...

STAR FACT

Stonefish are tough survivors, with thick, leathery skin to resist wounds from sharp rocks and sea urchin spines.

MY STAR RATING

SPECIAL FEATURES

EYES AND MOUTH: The eyes and mouth are on top of the head facing upwards, so the stonefish can keep a constant watch on prey passing above.

VENOM: Thirteen short, sharp spines on the fish's back pierce and inject venom into any creature that tries to attack.

SUN BATHER

Despite eating mainly jellyfish, squid and similar soft-bodied creatures, the ocean sunfish grows to be the world's largest bony fish. (This group includes all fish with bony skeletons – not cartilage-skeleton sharks.) After diving deep into colder water to feed, the sunfish lives up to its name by lying on its side at the water's surface to soak up the warmth of the Sun's rays.

Sunfish

Scientific name: Mola mola
Type: Fish
Lifespan: 10–12 years
Height: 3 m
Weight: Up to 1.5 tonnes
Range: Worldwide except cold and polar seas
Status: Not assessed

LET'S GO...

Lacking a proper tail, the sunfish 'rows' along by waving its dorsal (upper) and anal (lower) fins from side to side like oars.

STAR FACT

The adult sunfish's extreme size makes it too big for most ocean predators, except large sharks and killer whales.

SPECIAL FEATURES

SKIN: The tough skin is up to 6 cm thick and is covered by tiny tooth-like denticles rather than the usual scales.

MOUTH: The sunfish's teeth are fused (joined) into a strong 'beak' that is suited to cutting up both floppy, squidgy jellyfish and hard shellfish.

No other creatures can survive the conditions that emperor penguins endure. Huddled in an Antarctic gale, they face stinging snow and wind-chill of −50°C. These flightless fish-hunters waddle more than 80 kilometres inland to their breeding site. After mating, the females return to the ocean to hunt, while the males stand together, each keeping an egg warm on his feet. Nine weeks pass before the chick hatches and the well-fed female returns to take over the care.

BLIZZARD BIRD

Emperor penguin

Scientific name: *Aptenodytes forsteri*
Type: Bird
Lifespan: 20–25 years, rarely 40-plus
Height: 1.2 m
Weight: 30–40 kg
Range: Antarctica
Status: Least concern

STAR FACT

Over the course of the journey inland, courtship, caring for the egg and chick, and finally travelling back to the sea to feed, the male's body weight may decrease by 50 percent, from 40 to 20 kg.

SHIVER...

After the females leave, the males gather in close groups to share body warmth. They take turns braving the outside and sheltering on the inside.

WARMTH: The penguin's copious layers of feathers keep its body at a snug 39°C, helped by a 3-cm-thick fatty layer of blubber under the skin.

HUDDLING: The temperature in the middle of an emperor penguin huddle can be more than 70°C higher than on the outer edge.

VOCAL CALLS: A courting couple call loudly to each other. When the female returns from the sea, nine weeks after laying, she locates her mate by calling for him.

DIVING: When the penguins return to the sea they hunt, diving for 20 minutes at a time to depths of 500 m to restock their body food reserves with fish.

FOOT SOLDIER

Army ant colonies are constantly on the move, marching along tropical forest floors. All the ants within the colony serve the lead ant – the queen – and do different jobs to ensure the colony's survival. Army ants have no permanent home – at night they form a temporary shelter (bivouac) out of their own bodies to protect the queen and her larvae (young). Any small creatures that stray into the colony's path, such as beetles, other ants, mice, lizards and baby birds, are bitten and stung to death, torn into bits and eaten.

YUM...

Workers cut up and carry pieces of food back to the main colony for the larvae, soldiers and queen.

SPECIAL FEATURES

NUMBERS: Small army ant colonies number a few thousand, but a big group may have more than one million individuals.

SWARMING: If a few ants find food or get into a fight, they release chemical messages called pheromones. In seconds, thousands come to help.

Army ant

Scientific name: *Eciton* and others
Type: Insect
Lifespan: Workers 3–12 months, queens 10-plus years
Length: Workers 5–10 mm, soldiers 20-plus mm
Range: Most tropical regions
Status: Least concern

ATTACK ...

A soldier ant's extremely long, curved, pointed jaws (visible just below the feelers) are called mandibles, and work like stabbing pincers.

STAR FACT

Soldier army ants have such outsized mouthparts that they cannot feed themselves, so the worker ants do this chore.

MY STAR RATING

FEARLESSNESS: The soldiers act by instinct and have no fear. They have no problem attacking enemies that are thousands of times larger than themselves.

DIGESTION: Powerful chemicals in the ant's venom and digestive system can dissolve almost any part of any animal victim, even horns and hooves.

A champion of extremes for many reasons, the ostrich is the tallest, heaviest and fastest-running of all birds. It also lays the biggest eggs and may have the widest diet. Plant foods such as leaves, grasses, shoots, seeds and fruits are its mainstay. But a hungry ostrich snaps up worms, spiders and insects such as beetles and locusts as well as scavenging, vulture-like, on the kills of predators such as lions and hyaenas.

BIGGEST BIRDIE

KEEPING WATCH...

The grey-brown female keeps her eggs warm and guarded by day, well camouflaged against dry plants and earth. At night the black-feathered male takes over.

FEET: The huge feet have only two toes each, compared to four on most other birds. The inner toe has a formidable claw for slashing enemies.

LEGS: The leg design is typical of a speedy mover, with most of the muscle bulk high in the hip region, and a very long shin.

Ostrich

Scientific name: *Struthio camelus*
Type: Bird
Lifespan: 40 years, rarely more
Height: 2–2.2 m
Weight: Up to 140 kg
Range: Africa south of the Sahara
Status: Least concern

STAR FACT

The ostrich egg is the world's biggest, at 15 cm long and 13 cm wide, and weighing 1.5 kg. Yet it is one of the smallest eggs in proportion to the body size of the bird that lays it.

RUN ...

A panicked ostrich can reach speeds of more than 70 km/h as it tries to escape danger – and can keep running for an hour or more.

MY STAR RATING

GUTS: The ostrich swallows up to one kg of pebbles into its first gut compartment, the muscular gizzard, to helps its digestive system grind up tough plant matter.

SIGHT: Huge eyes, each 5 cm across, allow the ostrich to see extreme details both at a distance and up close.

SPRINT CHAMP

A young springbok raises its head to sniff and look around – and sees a cheetah rocketing towards it. This big cat must catch its quarry within 30 seconds, or its body will overheat from the extreme effort required to bound along faster than any other land animal. The springbok tries to zig-zag but the cheetah responds, swishing its tail from side to side to aid its sudden fast turns. The cheetah rapidly bowls over the springbok, clamps its jaws onto the victim's windpipe, and waits for its struggle to subside.

GOTCHA...

When it is within striking distance the cheetah extends a front leg and hooks a claw into its prey to trip it up.

STAR FACT

'Tear stripes' – thin black lines that extend from the inside of each eye to the corner of the mouth – may work like anti-glare sunglasses to help the cheetah see in the fierce midday sun.

SPECIAL FEATURES

BUILD: The cheetah is slim, lightweight and long-legged. Most of its muscle bulk is in the shoulders and hips, to move its limbs.

FLEXIBILITY: The bendy backbone arches up as the cheetah's legs extend front and rear, then curves down as the legs come together under it.

Cheetah

Scientific name: *Acinonyx jubatus*
Type: Mammal
Lifespan: 10–12 years
Length: Head-body 1.2 m, tail 80 cm
Weight: 40–60 kg
Range: North, east and southern Africa
Status: Vulnerable

LAUNCH...

Hurling itself from the cover of a bush, the cheetah lowers its small head for extra streamlining, extends its claws for a better grip on the ground, and the race is on.

ACCELERATION: From standstill to 100 km/h takes a cheetah just three seconds, an incredible rate that few prey animals can match.

TOP SPEED: Cheetahs have been clocked running at speeds of more than 100 km/h, and in very short bursts as fast as 120 km/h.

Forget the lion, tiger, bear, great white and killer whale – the world's largest predator by far is the sperm whale, and it is heavier than all those others combined. This massive monster has titanic deep-sea battles with its prey, the world's largest invertebrate, the giant squid. The sperm whale holds other records too: it has the world's biggest brain, at 8 kilograms (six times bigger than our own), and it undertakes the longest, deepest dives of any air-breathing animal.

GIANT HUNTER

TIME TO DIVE...

Raising its massive tail flukes above the surface means that the sperm whale is about to head straight down into the blackness of the ocean depths.

SPECIAL FEATURES

DIVING: This whale's muscles and blood have many more microscopic oxygen-storing cells and substances than those found in other animals.

BREATHING: At the surface, the whale takes a huge breath every 10–12 seconds. Breathing out sends a steamy fountain 15 m into the air.

Sperm whale

Scientific name: *Physeter macrocephalus*
Type: Mammal
Lifespan: 60–70 years
Length: Male 20 m, female 13 m
Weight: Male 50 tonnes, female 20 tonnes
Range: All oceans
Status: Vulnerable

BIG HEAD ...

The whale's huge forehead is mostly full of a waxy oil known as spermaceti. This may alter the animal's buoyancy (ability to float), helping it to descend and then return to the surface.

STAR FACT

By tracking individual sperm whales, scientists have learnt that these mammals can dive below 3000 m and stay underwater for 90 minutes.

TEETH: The teeth are only visible in the lower jaw, with about 20–25 on each side. In the upper jaw they are small and remain below the gum surface.

FOREHEAD: The spermaceti in the head may also help to focus sound waves, which might play a part in the whale's echolocation navigation system.

As dusk falls in the rainforest, it's time for the fruit bat colony to wake up, yawn and groom themselves with claws and teeth. They flap along from their daytime roost to the feeding area, which could be as far as 70 kilometres away, on their extremely long wings. Here they cluster around the latest ripe fruits and begin to lick, nibble, suck and chew to extract the soft pulp and juices, then spit out the hard, stringy bits.

FRUITY FLAPPER

Spectacled fruit bat

Scientific name: *Pteropus conspicillatus*
Type: Mammal
Lifespan: 12–15 years
Length: Male 25 cm, female 22 cm
Weight: Male 900 g, female 700 g
Range: New Guinea, northeast Australia
Status: Least concern

WOW...

A lever mechanism in the bat's foot bones means that when it hangs, its toes automatically curl around so that it grips the perch with hardly any effort.

STAR FACT

The fruit bat's long muzzle, used for smelling ripe fruits, and big ears, give it the common name of flying fox.

SPECIAL FEATURES

SIGHT: Big, sensitive eyes mean the spectacled fruit bat can see well to fly and feed in the dark, except on cloudy, moonless nights.

WINGS: With a span of more than 110 cm, the wings are held out by extremely long, thin finger bones. The claw is the thumb.

ETERNAL FLIER

The Arctic tern is the world's greatest animal traveller, and never sees winter. It breeds in the far north around the Arctic during summer, then spends three months flying from the top to the bottom of the world, arriving at the far south of Antarctica – where it is also summer. After a few months of rest and refuelling, it's time to complete its giant round trip and return to the Arctic, and the cycle starts all over again.

STAR FACT

Each migration may be 20,000 km. A lifetime of lengthy flights means an Arctic tern may travel a distance equivalent to a return journey to the Moon.

Arctic tern

Scientific name: *Sterna paradisaea*
Type: Bird
Lifespan: 25–30 years
Length: 35 cm
Weight: 110 g
Range: Arctic and Antarctic (migrates between the two)
Status: Least concern

KEEP OUT...

Arctic terns defend their nests by diving at intruders, calling loudly and even swooping down to peck, or release foul-smelling fluids.

SPECIAL FEATURES

STAMINA: This tern's extraordinary migration takes from two to four months, snatching quick snacks from the ocean surface along the route.

BEAK: The tern flutters and then dips down to the surface or even plunges in, to grasp fish with its long, slim, ridge-edged beak.

In the depths of winter, when snow carpets the ground and lakes freeze solid, relaxing in a hot tub might seem a human luxury. But the macaques of Japan, sometimes called 'snow monkeys', have taken to bathing in the natural hot springs scattered across the country. These are the most northern-dwelling of all monkeys and apes (apart from humans), and they cope with extremes of temperature as low as –15°C in winter and up to 30°C in summer.

SNOWY SPA BATHER

CLEVER...

Parent macaques teach their young how to feed, bathe, and generally survive during an extended infancy of more than two years.

SPECIAL FEATURES

DIET: The macaque's foods change with the seasons, from bark and buds in winter, to shoots and flowers in spring, then fruits in autumn.

HANDS: The monkey's thumb is opposable, like our own, able to grip and manipulate foods and other objects very precisely.

Japanese macaque

Scientific name: *Macaca fuscata*
Type: Mammal
Lifespan: 25–30 years
Length: Head-body 70 cm, tail 10 cm
Weight: Males up to 12 kg, females up to 9 kg
Range: Islands of Japan
Status: Least concern

STAR FACT

In some troops of Japanese macaques, the monkeys have been observed pressing snow into balls with their hands, then rolling the snowball along to make it larger – seemingly just for fun.

ME FIRST ...

In macaque troops, females outnumber males and have a hierarchy, or pecking order, showing who is boss. The chief or dominant individuals get first choice of the best places in the hot spring.

FUR: The macaque's warm fur coat grows even thicker in winter to protect it from the worst of the winds, rain and snow in their upland habitats.

INTELLIGENCE: The clever Japanese macaque quickly picks up new tricks, and has learnt to wash sand or mud off its food before eating.

SALTY SURVIVOR

A constant hubbub of low squawks, grunts and even cow-like mooing make the flamingo nesting colony a busy place. Thousands of these tall, long-necked, stilt-legged wading birds arrive, leave and jostle for space among the volcano-like mounds of mud that are their nests. Some of the lakes where lesser flamingoes set up colonies are so hot and caustic (salty) that they would burn human skin. But the unconcerned birds wade easily and feed hungrily, stopping occasionally to preen their pink plumage.

The newly hatched chick has stumpy legs and a short, straight beak. It does not gain its spindly adult proportions until it is one year old.

CUTE ...

SPECIAL FEATURES

LEGS: The flamingo has the extremely long, thin legs of a wading bird, allowing it to walk safely in water more than 40 cm deep.

FEET: The bird's wide-toed webbed feet are ideal for walking on soft mud or sand. The tough skin resists water temperatures of more than 40°C.

AWESOME ...

Colonies of more than two million lesser flamingoes crowd the highly salty lakes of east Africa.

Lesser flamingo

Scientific name: *Phoenicopterus minor*
Type: Bird
Lifespan: Up to 50 years
Height: 90–100 cm
Weight: 2 kg
Range: Africa, southern Asia
Status: Near threatened

STAR FACT

The flamingo feeds on tiny, plant-like life-forms called blue-green algae. The algae provide substances that the bird alters within its body to give its feathers their pink colour.

MY STAR RATING

NECK: Long legs raise the body up high, but the equally elongated neck compensates so the bird can easily reach down to its foot level to feed.

BILL: The deep, angled beak has rows of comb-like ridges inside. These work as filters to strain tiny plants, and also small shrimps and worms, from the water.

Snuffle, probe, feel, catch, bite, swallow! In less than half a second the star-nosed mole can locate, identify and eat a small prey item. This mini-mole, which could fit in an adult's hand, is an expert predator both underground and underwater. It gobbles up any small creatures, including worms, bugs, tadpoles, small fish, shrimps and little shellfish. Its star feature is its star-shaped nose, which is extremely sensitive to touch and taste as well as smell.

STARRY SWIMMER

STAR FACT

The star organ is a ring of 22 fleshy, bendy, finger-like tentacles, its total size about as wide as your fingernail. Each tentacle can move on its own to touch and feel with incredible accuracy.

QUICK ...

The multi-purpose front feet are spades for digging in earth, paddles for swimming and levers for moving underwater rocks to find prey.

SPECIAL FEATURES

FUR: The thick double-coat of fur repels water so the mole does not get waterlogged and cold on its underwater expeditions.

SMELL: Underwater, the mole can breathe bubbles of air out of its nose onto interesting objects, then breathe them in again to detect any smell.

Star-nosed mole

Scientific name: *Condylura cristata*
Type: Mammal
Lifespan: 2–4 years
Length: Up to 20 cm
Weight: 50 g
Range: Eastern North America
Status: Least concern

The star-nosed mole is on the go day and night, needing big meals every few hours. It must eat enough to keep its little body warm and fuel its hyperactive lifestyle.

FRONT FEET: Like most moles, this species uses its powerful, massive-clawed front feet to dig burrows, both to live in and when foraging for food.

TAIL: During times of plentiful food the mole's tail grows thicker with stored fat, which is used later as an energy reserve when prey is scarce.

SEAWEED EATER

Marine iguanas are found only on the Galapagos Islands. They are also the only lizards that regularly dive into salty water, and the only reptiles to eat just seaweeds and similar plants. Although they lie on the Equator, the seas around the Galapagos are surprisingly chilly, at 22–24°C. After each dive for food, the iguana must sit on a seaside rock to warm itself before it can venture back into the cool water. Each lizard has its own favoured patch of rock as its territory, which it jealously defends against intruders.

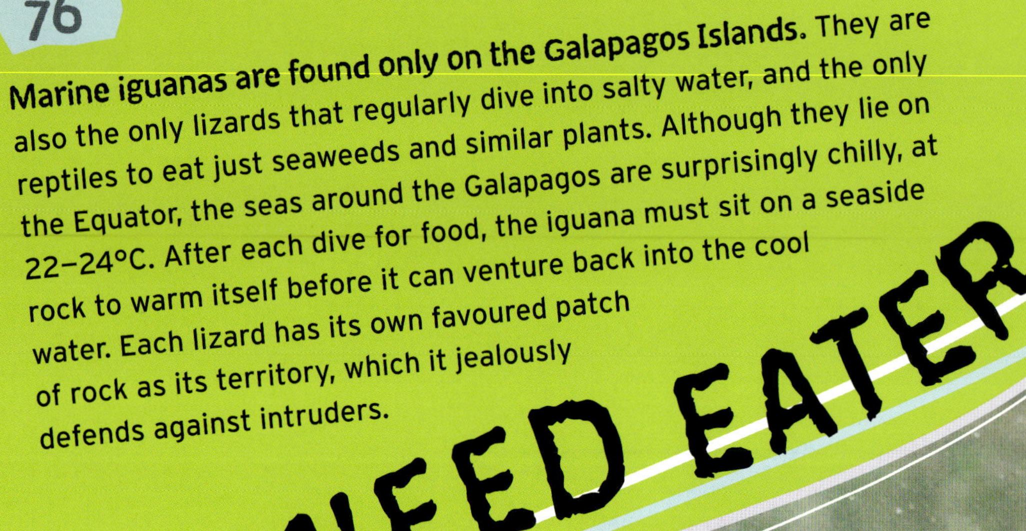

STAR FACT

Special glands in the iguana's nose collect unwanted salt from its food. The lizard then sneezes out the salt, which often ends up as a pile of white crystals on its head.

SPECIAL FEATURES

DIVING: Marine iguanas can dive to depths of 15 m, lasting for 30 minutes on one breath of air. Deeper than this the water is too cold and dark.

SNOUT: Its short, blunt snout allows the marine iguana to scrape off the newest, most nutritious seaweeds or algae coating the rocks.

The iguana nibbles fresh seaweed growths from the submerged rocks using its small but very sharp teeth.

Galapagos marine iguana

Scientific name: *Amblyrhynchus cristatus*
Type: Reptile
Lifespan: 20 years
Length: Male up to 1.5 m, female 1 m
Weight: 1–2 kg
Range: Galapagos Islands (Pacific Ocean)
Status: Vulnerable

When iguanas first emerge from the sea they are so cold that they cannot run away if threatened, so they are very ready to bite enemies.

CLAWS: The iguana's claws are long, curved and sharp, to grip slippery rocks both when feeding under the surface and clambering over them when above.

TAIL: The long tail is both tall and narrow from side to side, like that of a crocodile – ideal for powerful swimming when the iguana swishes it from side to side.

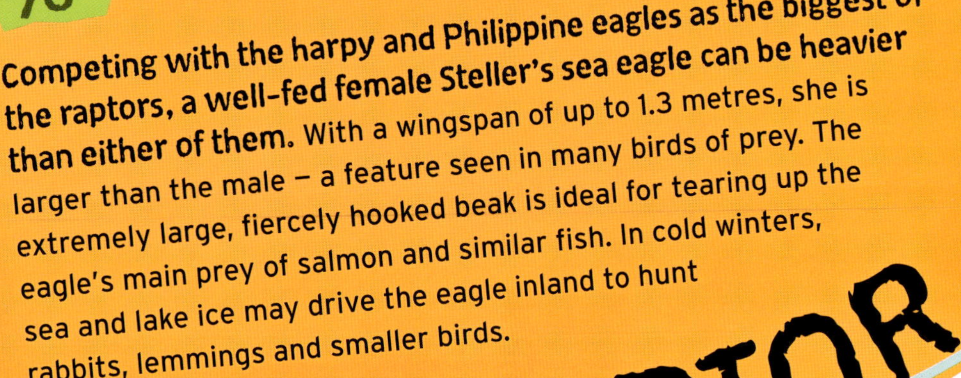

Competing with the harpy and Philippine eagles as the biggest of the raptors, a well-fed female Steller's sea eagle can be heavier than either of them. With a wingspan of up to 1.3 metres, she is larger than the male – a feature seen in many birds of prey. The extremely large, fiercely hooked beak is ideal for tearing up the eagle's main prey of salmon and similar fish. In cold winters, sea and lake ice may drive the eagle inland to hunt rabbits, lemmings and smaller birds.

FISHY RAPTOR

STAR FACT

Far from being a noble hunter, this eagle may be a sneaky kleptoparasite (a creature that robs other animals of their meals). It chases and attacks other birds, forces them to drop or cough up any food they have, and then it eats it.

SWOOP...

The sea eagle circles several metres above the water's surface, scanning for signs of fish below such as ripples, bubbles, shadowy movements or exposed fins.

SPECIAL FEATURES

SIZE: The largest aerial hunter in its region, an adult Steller's sea eagle is too big to be attacked by other birds, or by many mammals either.

FEET: The long, scale-covered toes and extremely sharp talons are adapted for gripping slippery, slimy, struggling fish.

Steller's sea eagle

Scientific name: *Haliaeetus pelagicus*
Type: Bird
Lifespan: 20–25 years
Length: Male 90 cm, female 100 cm
Weight: Male 5 kg, female 8 kg
Range: Coasts on northeast Asia
Status: Vulnerable

Apart from the breeding season, Steller's sea eagles usually live and hunt alone. If food is scarce they may gather at a source such as a whale carcass and fight over the remains.

BEAK: The typical bird-of-prey hooked beak has exceptionally sharp edges and a tightly curved tip, suited to slicing through a fish's scaly skin.

FEATHERS: The sea eagle's home area has long, cold winters, so the bird's plumage is extra-thick with very fluffy down feathers under the outer layer.

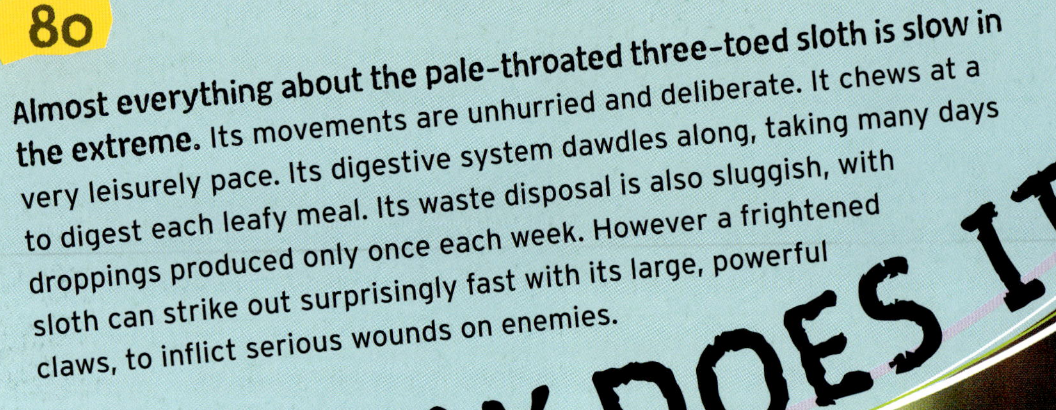

Almost everything about the pale-throated three-toed sloth is slow in the extreme. Its movements are unhurried and deliberate. It chews at a very leisurely pace. Its digestive system dawdles along, taking many days to digest each leafy meal. Its waste disposal is also sluggish, with droppings produced only once each week. However a frightened sloth can strike out surprisingly fast with its large, powerful claws, to inflict serious wounds on enemies.

SLOWLY DOES IT

YAWN ...

Sloths either rest, doze or sleep for up to 18 hours each day. They are able to hang on in their treetop homes even when deeply asleep.

Pale-throated sloth

Scientific name: *Bradypus tridactylus*
Type: Mammal
Lifespan: 12–15 years
Length: 50 cm
Weight: 4 kg
Range: Forests of Central and South America
Status: Least concern

STAR FACT

Unlike other mammals, sloths allow their body temperature to vary with their surroundings. When it gets cold, they get even slower!

SPECIAL FEATURES

CLIMBING: Three long claws on each foot dig deep into bark, allowing the sloth to cling securely to a trunk or hang upside down from a bough.

CAMOUFLAGE: Tiny plants and mosses grow in grooves and pits in the sloth's fur, giving it extremely accurate camouflage.

WEIRD ANIMALS

SUPER STRANGE

What huge ears! Look at those bizarre horns! Odd feet, strange noses, peculiar tails... some animals are very weird indeed, and quite unlike other creatures.

Animals have unusual features for good reasons. In the wild, anything that gives an advantage over rivals may be key to survival. So really big ears may catch the faintest sounds to locate food, while spines or armour protect against predators.

Other features may be used to attract and impress potential mates. When creatures get together at breeding time, what seems really weird to us looks totally appealing to their own kind.

Very slowly, the chameleon creeps along the branch, relying on its incredibly tiny movements and amazing camouflage to remain unnoticed by its insect prey. This strangest of lizards rocks its body slightly to gauge distance with its swivelling eyes. Then, faster than the human eye can follow, it flicks out its immensely long, slimy tongue. The fly is caught on the sticky, suction-cup tip, and the chameleon leisurely chews its latest meal.

HORNED MONSTER

STAR FACT

Most chameleons lay eggs, but Jackson's chameleon gives birth to live young. Within hours of being born the babies are practising their hunting skills on tiny prey such as mosquitoes.

DOWN IN ONE...

This Namaqua desert chameleon has just caught a beetle. Its sticky tongue flicks into its mouth and the hard-cased, spiky victim will be crushed, slurped and swallowed in seconds.

SPECIAL FEATURES

HORNS: The male's horns are mostly for show, to frighten enemies and impress females when breeding, but they can be jabbed at attackers.

CAMOUFLAGE: Chameleons can change colour. The colours indicate moods such as anger or fright, and are sometimes for camouflage, too.

Jackson's chameleon

Scientific name: *Chamaeleo jacksonii*
Type: Reptile
Lifespan: 3–5 years
Length: 30 cm
Weight: Up to 500 g
Range: East Africa
Status: Not assessed

WOW...

Each eye turret swivels through almost a full half circle, independent of the other eye, so the chameleon can look to the front and rear at the same time!

MY STAR RATING

TONGUE: A typical chameleon has a tongue about two-thirds as long as its body. It can flick out, catch prey on its sticky tip and return in one-fifth of a second.

FEET: The weird feet each have five toes that are fused (joined) into two groups of two and three, like a pincer, to give excellent branch-gripping power.

This strange fish gulps in water to make its body swell up, becoming as round and hard as a football. Once it has done so, predators will have problems even getting a bite of the porcupinefish, never mind trying to swallow it. The sharp, thorn-like growths in its skin usually lie flat against its body. But as the fish swells, the spines tilt and start to poke outwards, putting off the predator even more.

SPIKY SWIMMER

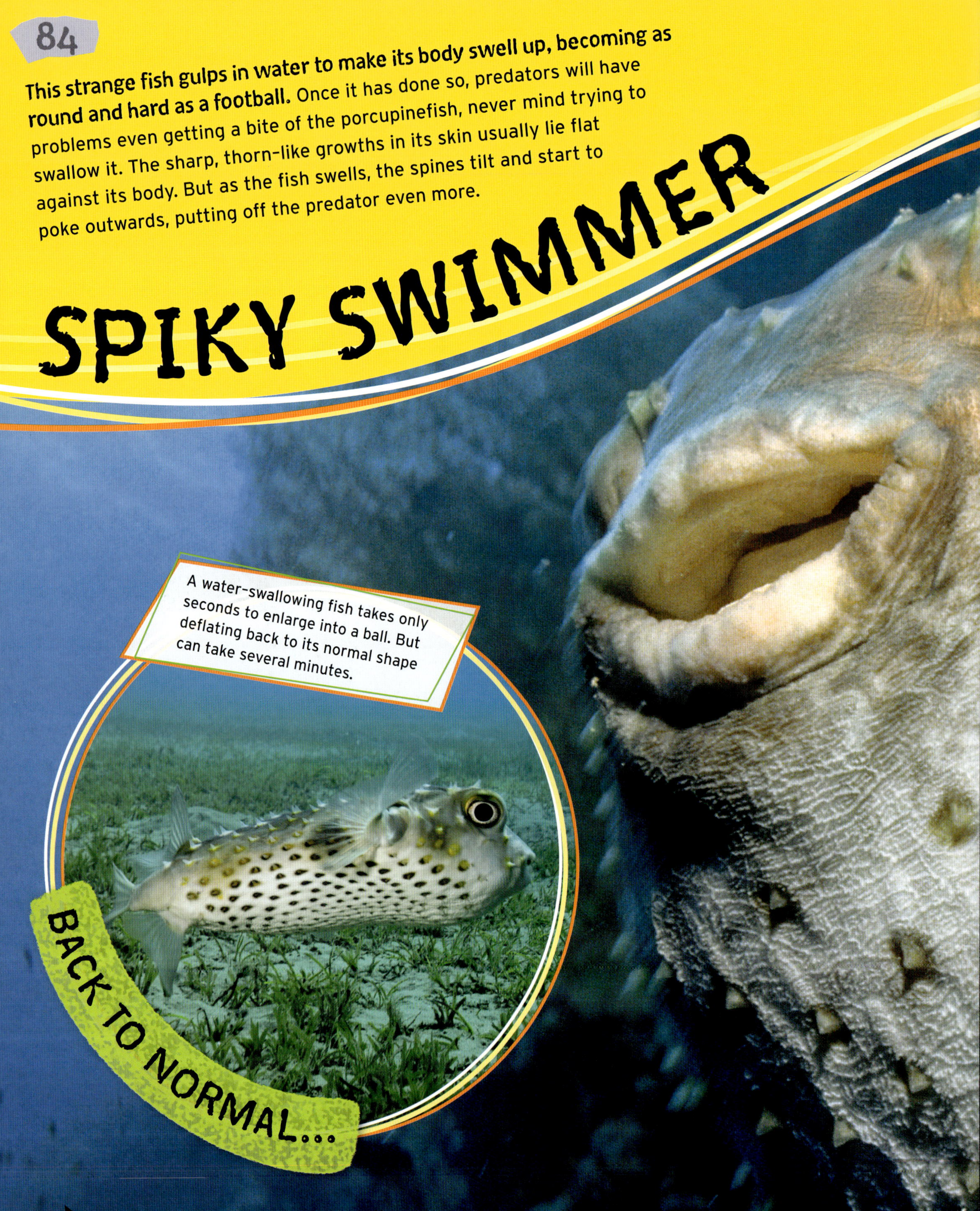

A water-swallowing fish takes only seconds to enlarge into a ball. But deflating back to its normal shape can take several minutes.

BACK TO NORMAL...

SPECIAL FEATURES

SWIMMING: Porcupinefish and their relatives are very agile swimmers, moving sideways and even backwards as they forage for food.

BEAK: A porcupinefish's teeth are solidly fused into a hard, strong beak that can crush prey such as sea-snails, clams and mussels.

Porcupinefish

Scientific name: *Cyclichthys* (several species)
Type: Fish
Lifespan: Unknown in the wild
Length: 20 cm
Weight: 100–150 g
Range: Southeast Atlantic, Indian and West Pacific Oceans
Status: Not assessed

STAR FACT

Many porcupinefish hide in cracks in the reef, and in the chambers inside sponges (large marine animals without backbones) during the day, emerging at night to feed.

OUCH...

The fish's strong protective spines have very sharp tips. They are made from a material similar to that of the rods or rays that hold out and wave the fins.

MY STAR RATING

EYES: Its large eyes are adapted for seeing in the dark, as this porcupinefish is nocturnal. It hunts over mud and sand and also among reef rocks and corals.

SKIN: The spines are fixed into strong, tough skin that is also stretchy enough to allow the fish to expand as it 'puffs up' with water.

As the heat and light fade on the dry African grasslands, a strange creature shuffles and snorts inside its 12-metre-long burrow. The aardvark's long nose resembles that of an anteater, and its excellent senses of hearing and smell are tuned to the tiny scrabbling sounds and scent of the insects that make up nearly all of its diet – ants and termites. Hungry after a day's sleep, on a good night the aardvark's long, snake-like tongue will lick up more than 50,000 of its tiny prey.

DIGGER CHAMP

The aardvark shelters in its burrow by day, and emerges at dusk to begin its night of foraging.

SPECIAL FEATURES

FUR AND SKIN: A furry coat of coarse hairs, plus tough leathery skin, provide good protection while burrowing and against predators.

FEET AND CLAWS: The feet have big claws that resemble a combination of nail and hoof, for breaking into the hardest of termite mounds.

STAR FACT
The name aardvark means 'earth pig' in the Afrikaans language, but this animal's close relations actually include elephants and manatees (sea cows) rather than pigs.
Aardvark
Scientific name: Orycteropus afer
Type: Mammal
Lifespan: 10–15 years
Length: 2 m
Weight: 50–60 kg
Range: Most of Africa south of the Sahara
Status: Least concern
SCRAM...
One of the fastest animal burrowers, an aardvark confronted by an enemy out in the open can dig its way out of danger, disappearing into the soil in a few seconds.
MY STAR RATING
TEETH: Its small jaws have only molar (cheek) teeth. These have an unusual layered structure, are quite soft and regrow continuously as they wear down.
NOSE: The very long snout houses exceptionally sensitive smell detectors, while the nostrils can close in a split second to prevent clogging with soil.

With the impact of a bullet and lightning speed, the brightly coloured mantis shrimp jabs out its club-like second legs to bash its hard-cased prey to bits. Sea snails, crabs, clams and similar shellfish, other types of shrimps and prawns – nothing can withstand one of nature's fastest, most forceful attacks. No wonder human divers who are unlucky enough to experience their bludgeoning blows refer to these shrimps as 'thumbsplitters'.

SHELL STRIKER

STAR FACT

Mantis shrimps are surprisingly clever creatures. They can remember the locations of hidden food, rather than just relying on sight and smell, and will even move obstacles to get at it.

SMASH AND GRAB...

After smashing the hermit crab's shell, the mantis shrimp simply pulls the poor creature from its hiding place, hits it repeatedly to subdue it, then starts to feast on its soft body.

SPECIAL FEATURES

LEGS: Three pairs of walking legs allow the shrimp to scuttle along quickly. The seven pairs behind them have paddle-like flaps for swimming.

HAMMERS: The second pair of limbs are like spring-loaded hammers that flick out with dizzying speed at both prey and predators.

Peacock mantis shrimp

Scientific name: *Odontodactylus scyllarus*
Type: Crustacean
Lifespan: Possibly 5–10 years
Length: Up to 25 cm
Weight: 500 g
Range: Indian and West Pacific Oceans
Status: Not enough information

With its deadly hammer-legs at the ready, folded in a manner similar to the praying mantis insect, the mantis shrimp eyes its next target – you!

EYES: Its mobile, stalked eyes have detailed colour vision and can judge distance accurately, so the shrimp relies mainly on sight when hunting.

ANTENNAE: Two pairs of long antennae detect objects by touch, sense water currents, and scent floating substances in a form of underwater smelling.

It is covered in spines and it eats ants, so the echidna is sometimes known as 'spiny anteater', and it is a very unusual kind of mammal. It lays eggs, like a bird. Its young develop in the female's pouch, like a kangaroo. In cold conditions it lowers its body temperature to just a few degrees above freezing, like a hibernating dormouse. And it can dig itself out of sight into the ground in seconds, like a mole.

PRICKLE-TOP

GO AWAY...

Just like a hedgehog, the echidna can roll into a spiky ball that few predators can undo.

SPECIAL FEATURES

FRONT CLAWS: Big foreclaws enable the echidna to dig burrows for shelter and to rip into hard-walled termite mounds and ant nests.

BACK CLAWS: The echidna uses its long, curved rear claws to groom or comb its fur and prickles, removing dirt and any pests, such as fleas.

Short-beaked echidna

Scientific name: *Tachyglossus aculeatus*
Type: Mammal
Lifespan: 40–45 years
Length: 40–45 cm
Weight: 3–4 kg
Range: Australia, New Guinea
Status: Least concern

SNOUT: Very long and narrow, the snout is excellent for smelling food. But the mouth is as small as this 'O', unable to bite, so the echidna relies on its...

TONGUE: The 20-cm-long tongue flicks in and out up to 100 times each minute. Its sticky coating picks up food such as ants and termites.

The fly scans the flower for danger. All seems clear so it lands, ready to sip sweet nectar. Then... *jump, kick, grab, stab!* As if from nowhere the camouflaged crab spider topples the fly with a well-aimed kick. Gripping the victim with its legs, the spider stabs its fangs into the fly's body and injects poison and digestive juices. These paralyze the victim and gradually turn its insides into soupy mush for the spider to suck up.

HIDDEN KILLER

Goldenrod crab spider

Scientific name: *Misumena vatia*
Type: Arachnid
Lifespan: Unknown, possibly 5 years
Length: Male 4 mm, female 11 mm
Range: Northern temperate lands
Status: Not enough information

STAR FACT

The goldenrod crab spider changes its body colour to match the colour of its chosen flower. Over the course of a few days, it could go from white, to yellow, to pale green.

BEWARE...

Much larger than the male, the female crab spider crouches among the petals of her flower, matching their colours in every detail.

MY STAR RATING

SPECIAL FEATURES

LEGS: Like all members of its group, crab spiders have eight legs, but these are unusual because they bend to give a sideways motion, like a real crab.

FANGS: The crab spider's fangs are long and slim, designed for piercing the exoskeletons (hard outer body casings) of a wide range of insects.

LONG NECK

Weevils are types of beetles and most have long snouts, but the giraffe weevil goes one better. The males of this species have enormously elongated necks. In the breeding season rival males face each other to gain females and win territories (areas in which they can live and breed). Females prefer longer-necked partners, so the parading males show off to impress, and be chosen.

Giraffe weevil

Scientific name: *Trachelophorus giraffa*
Type: Insect
Lifespan: Unknown, probably 1–2 years
Length: Up to 3 cm
Range: Madagascar
Status: Not enough information

ME, ME...

The male lifts and sticks out his amazing neck, and nods it up and down at the middle joint, to display his size and strength to any watching females.

STAR FACT

Giraffe weevils are usually found on one particular species of tree, where they feed and breed. For this reason, this type of tree is known as the giraffe weevil tree.

SPECIAL FEATURES

NECK: The female also has a fairly long neck. This helps when building her nest of rolled-up leaves, in which she lays her single egg.

WINGS: The weevil's front pair of wings are protective covers. The second pair of flimsy flying wings are folded beneath them.

This big, strong bird is probably named because its huge beak, or bill, looks similar to the horn of a cow. The hornbill's amazing bill is covered in keratin (a tough, lightweight material) and has many uses, from feeding and preening to pecking enemies, and the female uses it to mix chewed food and droppings into a paste. She uses this paste for a strange purpose – to wall off the entrance to her nest hole, trapping herself inside. Only a narrow slit is left, through which the male passes food and she ejects droppings.

MEGA BEAK

The male hornbill supplies all of the female's food while she is trapped inside the nest hole.

SPECIAL FEATURES

FLIGHT: Despite their large size, hornbills fly strongly on their long, powerful wings, with noisy, whooshing wingbeats.

NECK: The two uppermost neck bones are joined or fused, and the neck has very strong muscles, so the bird can move its huge bill very accurately.

STAR FACT

The female hornbill is sealed inside her nest hole for more than one month, incubating her two or three eggs and then looking after the chicks once they have hatched.

Knobbed hornbill

Scientific name: *Aceros cassidix*
Type: Bird
Lifespan: 25–30 years
Length: 80–90 cm
Weight: 2 kg
Range: Southeast Asia, mainly Sulawesi
Status: Least concern

YUMMY...

With expert precision the hornbill plucks small berries, seeds, buds and similar items, ready to toss them up in the air and swallow them.

MY STAR RATING

SIGHT: Its two eyes face partly forwards and can see along the tapering bill to its tip, which allows the hornbill to peck and pick up food with great precision.

BILL: The hugely useful beak, and the red casque (ridge) on top, are not quite as heavy as they look, being partly honeycomb-like with air spaces inside.

One of nature's weirdest sights is a frightened frilled lizard trying to scare off an enemy. The lizard gapes its mouth wide and erects the wide frill of skin around its neck to make itself look bigger and more menacing. It also stands up stiff-legged and swishes its tail, hissing loudly. This defensive display makes most predators think twice. As they do so, the lizard suddenly turns tail, races away and leaps to safety in the branches of a nearby tree.

FRILLED DEFENDER

RACE...

Its long, muscular back legs carry the frilled lizard along almost as fast as you could run, but only for a short distance.

SPECIAL FEATURES

CAMOUFLAGE: Dull browns and greens give the frilled lizard excellent camouflage in its woodland habitat.

MOUTH: The wide mouth has small but strong teeth to grab and chew beetles, cicadas, ants and similar, small-but-tough prey.

Frilled lizard

Scientific name: *Chlamydosaurus kingii*
Type: Reptile
Lifespan: 10–15 years
Length: 90 cm
Weight: 500 g
Range: North Australia, New Guinea
Status: Least concern

STAR FACT

Frilled lizards hunt in trees for bugs such as caterpillars and spiders. They also prowl on the ground for insects, worms, and the occasional mouse, baby bird or smaller lizard.

HISS...

The brightly coloured frill, like a scaly umbrella, contrasts with the lizard's dull body colour. The frill measures up to 20 cm across.

MY STAR RATING

FRILL: The wide frill of leathery skin is held out by rods of gristle (cartilage). Usually it lies flat along the lizard's neck and shoulders.

FEET AND CLAWS: Very long toes and sharp, curved claws give the lizard great non-slip grip even on the smoothest, slipperiest bark.

SLICING SUCKER

Dusk falls and farm animals settle down to sleep. Then a shadow flits silently into the cowshed and lands on the ground – a vampire bat. With strange, scuttling movements it hops and scurries towards its victim. After a few seconds in which it snips away hairs to reach the cow's bare skin, the bat uses its sharp teeth to slice a neat, shallow, rounded wound, which starts to bleed. Special chemicals in its saliva keep the blood flowing, and the bat sets to work to suck and lap up its night-time snack.

During a 20–30 minute feed, a vampire bat may take in half of its own body weight in blood.

SPECIAL FEATURES

ECHOLOCATION: The vampire bat navigates in darkness by listening to the echoes of its own clicks and squeaks bouncing off nearby objects.

SIDE TEETH: The canine and molar teeth at the side and back of the mouth work like scissors to cut hair or fur that might interfere with feeding.

STAR FACT

If a vampire bat flies back to its roost still hungry, others in its colony may share their food, by regurgitating (bringing up) some of their own half-digested meals into its mouth!

SMILE...

Showing off its upper incisor (front) teeth, which are sharper than a cut-throat razor, a vampire bat gets ready for action.

Vampire bat

Scientific name: *Desmodus rotundus*
Type: Mammal
Lifespan: 8–11 years
Length: 9 cm
Weight: 50–80 g
Range: Central and South America
Status: Least concern

MY STAR RATING

FRONT TEETH: Like triangular blades, the upper incisor teeth are always sharp, ready to scoop away a small patch of skin and flesh.

SUCKING: This bat can lap up blood with its tongue or suck blood up using the underside of its tongue pressed down onto its lower lip.

DUCK-FACED DIVER

The platypus is famed for its strange features. It has a bill and webbed feet like a duck and lays eggs like a bird, but its furry body and wide, flat tail are more like those of a beaver. Perhaps even stranger is this Australian animal's 'sixth sense'. Its bill detects tiny pulses of electricity in the water given off by the moving muscles of its prey. So the platypus can find food by touch and electro-sense alone, even in the muddiest, darkest creeks and pools in the middle of the night!

'STAR FACT

Most platypus dives last 20–30 seconds, with occasional rests of a few minutes. Its main prey include worms, pond snails, shrimps, yabbies (crayfish), fish and frogs.

PHEW...

Eating one-fifth of your body weight every 24 hours is tiring. Platypuses swim and dive for food for up to 12 hours a day, usually from dusk until dawn.

SPECIAL FEATURES

TAIL: The wide, round-edged tail helps the rear feet in steering and braking. It also stores food reserves for times when prey is scarce.

FEET: Long, wide-splayed toes with webbed skin between them are ideal for paddling and swimming at the surface and underwater.

FUR: Its very dense fur traps tiny air bubbles that help the platypus to float upwards, as well as keeping its skin warm and dry.

BILL: The bill is slightly flexible, like thick rubber, and is amazingly sensitive to touch. The mouth is on the underside of the bill.

The armadillo looks like no other living creature. Although it resembles a scaly, plant-eating reptile from the age of dinosaurs, it's actually a warm-blooded mammal. It has fur poking out around the sides of its bony armour, and is a meat-eater of sorts, although its main foods are tiny termites, ants, worms and similar creepy-crawlies. It may also snack occasionally on ripe fruits, shoots and buds, or even scavenge the remains of dead animals.

ARMOUR-DILLO

MOVE IT...

Armadillos trot along on the clawed tips of their front feet and the flat soles of their back feet.

STAR FACT

There are 20 different species (kinds) of armadillo, all in the Americas, but only a few, including the three-banded, can roll into a tight ball.

SPECIAL FEATURES

ARMOUR: Bony plates called scutes grow within the thickness of the armadillo's skin, covered by outer scales made from horny keratin.

ROLLING UP: The three-banded armadillo's armour is flexible enough for it to curl into a ball, tucking in the head against the tail.

Three-banded armadillo

Scientific name: *Tolypeutes tricinctus* (Brazilian species)
Type: Mammal
Lifespan: 15 years
Length: 45–50 cm
Weight: 1.5–2 kg
Range: Northern South America
Status: Vulnerable

HIDE...

After curling up in self defence, the armadillo waits for several minutes and then opens up slightly to peek out and check that all is clear.

CLAWS: The front feet have massive claws to dig up food, excavate burrows for resting and hiding, and to scratch or slash enemies.

SMELL: Eyesight is poor but the sense of smell is acute, and an armadillo at the surface can scent food down to 20 cm below in the soil.

In the strange world of the seahorse, it's the male who has the babies. The female lays her eggs into a pocket-like pouch on his belly, where they develop over a few weeks. Then the father 'gives birth', and 200 or more tiny seahorses emerge. This extraordinary animal has other oddities too. It is one of the slowest of all fish, using only its back fin to get about, and every morning, a male and female 'dance' together to strengthen their partnership.

FISHY HORSE

LOOK...

Each of its bulging eyes can move independently of the other, so the seahorse can look to the front and rear at the same time.

Pot-belly seahorse

Scientific name: Hippocampus *abdominalis*
Type: Fish
Lifespan: 7–10 years
Length: 35 cm
Range: Coasts of Australia and New Zealand
Status: Not enough information

STAR FACT

The pot-belly seahorse is a bit of a giant, at more than 30 cm long. Some species are smaller than this word: 'seahorse'.

SPECIAL FEATURES

TAIL: A curly prehensile (gripping) tail allows the seahorse to hold onto weeds and rocks so that it can rest and stay safe even in strong currents.

MOUTH: Its mouth is small and tube-like, but the seahorse is still a busy feeder and can swallow more than 5000 tiny morsels daily.

SLOW AND SLIMY

Sea slugs are among the brightest creatures in the ocean. Also called nudibranchs, they shine as if lit from within as they slime their way across rocks and corals. They are not too worried about predators because their glowing hues are warning colours, showing that their rubbery flesh tastes horrible and may even be poisonous. They spend their days sliding around reefs, feeding at leisure on sponges, and mating occasionally – it's a lazy life.

GLIDE...

A sea slug gets about in the same way as its cousins on land. Waves of rippling muscle contraction pass along its broad base (foot) from tail to head, inching it forwards.

Tryon's sea slug

Scientific name: *Risbecia tryoni*
Type: Mollusc
Lifespan: Unknown, possibly 1–2 years
Length: 6 cm
Range: West Pacific Ocean
Status: Not enough information

STAR FACT

Sometimes groups of Tryon's sea slugs travel and feed in single file, one after the other. This is known as 'tailgating'.

SPECIAL FEATURES

TENTACLES: Head tentacles have detectors that sense touch, water movements and currents, and chemical sensors for 'smelling' underwater.

TONGUE: Under the head is a tongue, called a radula, that has rows of hundreds of tiny teeth for rubbing at and rasping up food.

Naked mole rats are not moles or rats, but cousins of guinea pigs and porcupines. They spend almost their entire lives in darkness underground, so their eyes barely function. And they have an odd, insect-like way of breeding. Only the queen mole rat gives birth, and she only mates with two or three males. The rest of the 80-strong colony (group) are soldiers that fight enemies, and workers that dig tunnels to gather roots and similar underground plant food.

LIFE IN THE DARK

MUNCH...

Workers gnaw, nibble and bite at the hard, dry earth to make a network of tunnels that might extend more than 4 km in total length.

SPECIAL FEATURES

TEETH: The very long, sharp incisor (front) teeth grow continuously as they wear down and self-sharpen as they are used to dig and eat.

LIPS: Lips can close and seal around the teeth even when the mouth is open, so the mole rat does not swallow soil as it tunnels.

Naked mole rat

Scientific name: *Heterocephalus glaber*
Type: Mammal
Lifespan: 25 years, even 28
Length: Worker 9 cm, queen 12 cm
Weight: Worker 30 g, queen 60 g
Range: East Africa
Status: Least concern

STAR FACT

Newborn mole rats feed on their mother's milk. As the babies develop they move on to eating the droppings of other colony members until they are old enough for proper food.

Naked mole rats sleep jumbled in a heap in their main living chamber. They also roll around in their shared urine and droppings, so that they carry the smell of their colony.

LEGS: Short limbs are needed in the cramped burrow, but the legs are very flexible and the mole rat can shuffle backwards as fast as it goes forwards.

SKIN: The mole rat's skin is not quite 'naked', in that it has some small hairs, but it is very tough and loose for scraping through tunnels.

GOGGLE EYES

Constant moisture makes rainforests the ideal places for frogs of all kinds – especially tree frogs. Among the leaves, the Ecuador tree frog steadies itself on its sucker toes. The special 'fly detector' sensors in its huge, bulging eyes are able to spot the tiniest gnat as it buzzes past. In a flash, the frog's head seems to split in half as it opens its enormous mouth and flicks out its long tongue. The tasty morsel is grabbed by the tongue's sticky, curling tip, pulled into the wide-open jaws, and swallowed.

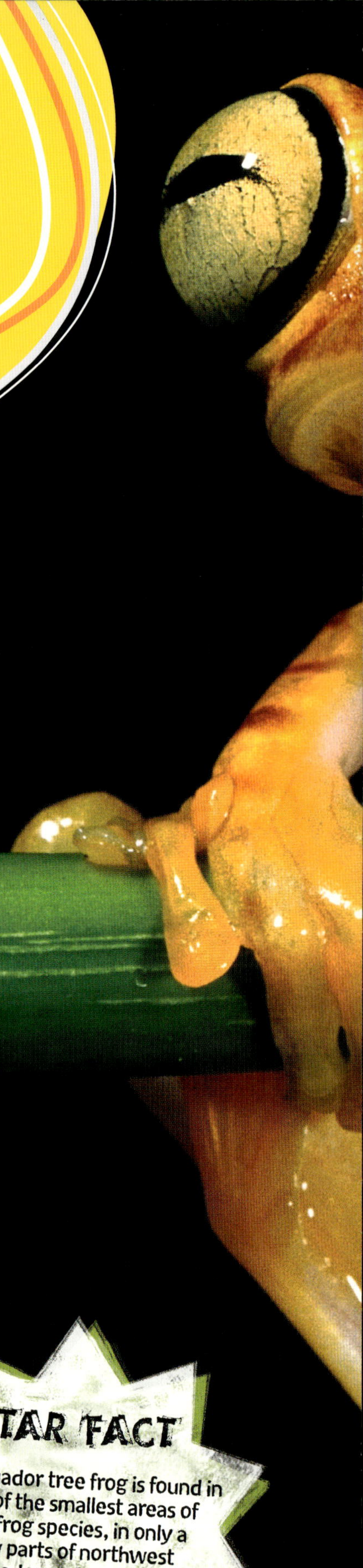

Male tree frogs make all kinds of croaks, whirrs, chirrups and burps to attract breeding partners.

RIBBIT...

STAR FACT

The Ecuador tree frog is found in one of the smallest areas of any frog species, in only a few parts of northwest Ecuador and southwest Colombia.

SPECIAL FEATURES

LIMBS: Despite its thinner-than-matchstick legs, this tree frog is surprisingly strong and can pull itself up using just one limb.

TOES: Large, sucker-like pads on the toe tips help to grip even the shiniest, slimiest, slipperiest rainforest leaves and twigs.

Ecuador tree frog

Scientific name: *Hypsiboas (Hyla) picturatus* (Ecuador, Imbabura or Chachi tree frog)
Type: Amphibian
Lifespan: Unknown, possibly 4–6 years
Length: 2–3 cm
Range: Northwest South America
Status: Least concern

The frog's mouth is the widest part of its head, ready to gulp in a meal that can be almost as big as the frog's own body.

MY STAR RATING

EYES: The frog's massive bulging eyes see even the tiniest movements and can also make out certain colours, even in the gloom cast by the forest canopy.

LEAPING: Its rear legs and feet are almost twice as long as the head and body, and have strong muscles for great leaps – usually to escape danger.

It may look like a regular lizard, but the tuatara is actually one of the weirdest of all creatures. Its close cousins were pig-sized, beak-mouthed reptiles called rhynchosaurs that lived alongside early dinosaurs more than 200 million years ago. The tuatara stays cool and lives life slowly. It takes more than 30 years to fully mature, it can hibernate for a year, its eggs may take 16 months to hatch, and some individuals might reach an amazing 150 years of age.

SLOWLY DOES IT

Tuatara

Scientific name: *Sphenodon* (two species)
Type: Reptile
Lifespan: Can exceed 100 years
Length: Male 60 cm, female 45 cm
Weight: Male 1 kg, female 0.5 kg
Range: New Zealand
Status: Vulnerable

COOL...

Most reptiles love to bask in temperatures of 25°C-plus warmth, but tuataras thrive best at 15–20°C. They are still active at 5°C, when most reptiles are too chilled to move.

SCALES: The tuatara's scaly plates have an odd structure, similar to a crocodile's plates. They are very tough, providing effective protection.

CREST: The crest of enlarged scales that runs from the head along the back is larger in males and can be held erect when displaying to females.

STAR FACT

If conditions are warm during egg development, more than about 21°C, most tuatara hatchlings are male. If it is cooler, below 19°C, they are female.

When it comes to meal times, tuataras are far from slow. They gulp down all kinds of smaller prey, from beetles and spiders to bird eggs and chicks, and even young tuataras!

GRAB AND GULP...

MY STAR RATING

THIRD EYE: Between the two main eyes the tuatara has the remains of a pineal or parietal 'third eye'. It detects light and dark but cannot form clear images.

TEETH: There are two rows of small teeth in the upper jaw and only one in the lower jaw, ideal for grabbing and chewing struggling victims.

The hoatzin has an abundance of bizarre features. Its body is plump and heavy but its head is tiny. It is a slow, clumsy flier, preferring to clamber among branches to find food. Its diet is mostly leaves, which are difficult to digest, so it has to consume huge amounts – up to one-quarter of its total weight is pecked-off leaves crammed into its guts. Oddest of all, the hoatzin chick has two claws on the front of each wing – a feature seen in prehistoric birds such as *Archaeopteryx* from the dinosaur age but in no other bird alive today.

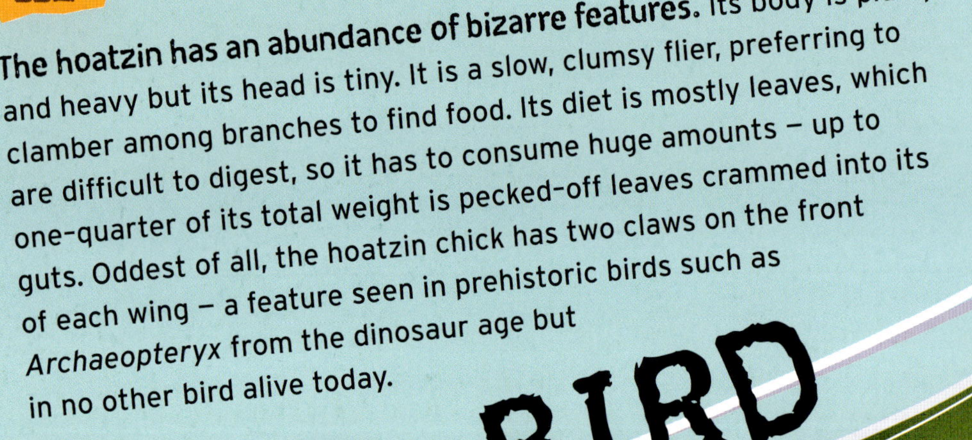

DINO-BIRD

MY TURN...

Hoatzin parent birds share the burden of raising their young. They take turns to incubate (keep warm) their two or three eggs and then feed the chicks.

HOLD ON...

The young hoatzin uses its wing claws, beak and feet to clamber about in the branches – and to climb back into its nest if it falls out.

SPECIAL FEATURES

FEATHERS: Life in the Amazon rainforest is very damp, but as the hoatzin preens it spreads lots of water-repelling oils onto its feathers.

CALLS: Hoatzins make many kinds of noises from hisses to grunts and loud screams. This helps members of a group to keep together.

STAR FACT

The way in which the hoatzin digests its green plant food inside its huge gut makes plenty of horrible-smelling gas, earning it the nickname of 'stinkbird'.

Hoatzin

Scientific name: *Opisthocomus hoazin*
Type: Bird
Lifespan: 20–25 years
Length: 60–70 cm
Weight: 800 g
Range: North-Central South America
Status: Least concern

ESCAPE: If a predator approaches, a hoatzin chick will fall out of its nest into the water below. Once danger passes, the chick swims to the bank and climbs back up.

DIGESTION: The enormous bag-like crop – the first part of the gut after the gullet – holds leaves for hours as they ferment (rot) and release their goodness.

Few insects are as strange to look at as the stalk-eyed fly. A close cousin of houseflies and mosquitoes, its body, wings and legs are fairly typical. But the head, especially in the males of the species, has enormously long rod-like stalks, one on each side, each with an eye and antenna (feeler) at the end. The stalks are so long that the distance between a fly's eyes may exceed its body length. Females are impressed by males with long stalks and choose them for breeding.

EYE-TO-FLY

STAR FACT

Long eye stalks are fragile, but as long as females keep choosing males with very wide eye spans, their offspring will continue to inherit the same extreme feature.

HEY, YOU...

Male stalk-eyed flies have eyeball-to-eyeball staring competitions. The one with the widest eye span wins and gets to breed.

SPECIAL FEATURES

LEGS: As well as eyeing up their rival's eye stalks, competing males spread out their front legs and may start to wrestle and kick each other.

EYE STALKS: In some kinds of stalk-eyed flies the male can force air from his mouth along tubes inside the stalks to make them even longer.

Stalk-eyed fly

Scientific name: *Teleopsis, Diopsis, Cyrtodiopsis* and others
Type: Insects
Lifespan: Mostly a few months
Length: 2–10 mm
Eyespan: 2–10 mm
Range: Mostly Africa, South and Southeast Asia
Status: Not assessed

Choosing a mate because of a certain body feature is known as sexual selection. Other examples include the male deer's large antlers and the male peacock's spectacular tail.

EYES: The eyes themselves are fairly normal (for a fly), with hundreds of tiny mosaic-like units that are very sensitive to movement.

MATING: Once a male fly has beaten his rivals, he may mate with up to 20 waiting females in just 20 minutes.

The proboscis monkey's nose is a normal size at birth – but it doesn't stay that way for long. It soon starts to grow much faster than the rest of the face. This is especially true of the males, and older male proboscis monkeys may have noses that hang down over their lips! This monkey also has a very limited diet. It feeds only on the leaves, shoots and seeds of the coastal mangrove trees in which it lives, which few other creatures are able to stomach.

BIG NOSE

Proboscis monkey

Scientific name: *Nasalis larvatus*
Type: Mammal
Lifespan: Unknown, probably 20 years
Length: Male 70 cm, female 60 cm
Weight: Male 20 kg, female 10 kg
Range: Borneo
Status: Endangered

STAR FACT

When these monkeys get excited, extra blood flows to the nose, so it becomes even bigger and redder!

FULL UP...

After a big meal, up to one-third of the monkey's body weight consists of partly chewed mangrove leaves crammed into its massive stomach.

MY STAR RATING

SPECIAL FEATURES

SWIMMING: Proboscis monkeys wade and swim very well in their seaside swamps – they even have partly webbed toes.

NOSE: The mega-nose acts as an amplifying chamber to make the monkey's calls louder, especially the alarm call that warns of danger.

ANIMAL GIANTS

BIG IS BEST

Millions of years ago, animal giants such as the dinosaurs *Diplodocus* and *Tyrannosaurus rex* roamed the Earth. Today there are other monster creatures living on our planet, including the biggest animal ever known – the blue whale.

Being big has advantages. Few animals dare to attack something bigger than themselves, and larger animals are likely to be stronger and able to reach food that others can't. But there are problems too. For example, a big animal needs to find and eat lots of food to have enough energy to survive.

Each animal group has its own giants, but size is relative. A giant hornet is far bigger than any similar species, but tiny compared to an albatross or a giant tortoise.

TRUNK AND TUSKS

The biggest of all land animals, the African elephant is enormously strong and powerful, but it can be surprisingly gentle too. Despite its great bulk, the elephant can move around almost silently and caresses its young with a soothing stroke of its trunk. But when frightened or angry, an elephant will bulldoze anything in its path while making loud trumpeting calls. Both male and female African elephants have huge tusks, which they use for digging up food and stripping bark from trees to eat.

BIG BABIES...

A newborn baby elephant can weigh as much as 120 kg – more than 30 times the weight of an average human baby – and is 1 m tall.

ON GUARD...

Elephant mums stay close to their young. Few predators dare to attack a baby elephant when mum, her giant tusks at the ready, is standing guard.

SPECIAL FEATURES

TRUNK: An elephant's trunk is its nose and upper lip all in one. It is used for smelling, drinking and lifting and is terrifically strong.

EARS: An elephant flaps its big ears to help cool itself down. It also flaps its ears when calling or listening to other elephants' calls.

African elephant

Scientific name: *Loxodonta africana*
Type: Mammal
Lifespan: About 60 years
Height: Male up to 4 m, female 3.4 m
Weight: Male up to 6.3 tonnes, female 3.5 tonnes
Range: Africa, south of the Sahara
Status: Near threatened

STAR FACT

An African elephant's tusks are actually very long front teeth. A male's tusks can be 2 m in length and each one can weigh more than 60 kg – that's as much as an adult human!

MY STAR RATING

FEET: An elephant's foot is like a big, spongy cushion with the toes buried inside. This shape helps spread the elephant's great weight.

APPETITE: A big elephant needs lots of food, munching through more than 150 kg of leaves, twigs, roots and fruit every day.

A few snake species beat the anaconda on length, but this snake's chunky coils make it the heaviest of all. It can weigh as much as three humans and grow longer than two cars parked end-to-end. Lurking in shallow water or on the forest floor, the anaconda waits for prey such as capybaras (giant rodents), peccaries (mammals similar to wild pigs) and caimans (alligator-like reptiles). When one wanders near, the snake seizes it, wraps its coils around its struggling body, and squeezes so tightly that the prey suffocates.

COLOSSAL COILS

STAR FACT

It can take an anaconda around six hours to swallow a large animal such as a capybara, which weighs around 45 kg. But after that, the snake won't need another meal for several months.

SPECIAL FEATURES

ADAPTATIONS: Eyes and nostrils positioned right on top of the head allow the anaconda to breathe and keep watch for prey while in water.

WIDE MOUTH: Stretchy jaws mean that the anaconda can open its mouth super-wide, allowing it to swallow prey larger than its own head.

Green anaconda

Scientific name: *Eunectes murinus*
Type: Reptile
Lifespan: 10 years, rarely up to 25
Length: 6–10 m, female longer and heavier than male
Weight: Up to 225 kg
Range: Northern South America
Status: Least concern

Despite its huge size, the anaconda's mottled colouration makes it hard to spot among dead leaves on the forest floor.

A full-grown anaconda can measure as much as 30 cm around its body – thicker than an adult man's arm.

SWIMMING: An excellent swimmer, the anaconda is able to hunt its prey in water just as expertly as it does on land.

GROWTH: From birth to full maturity an anaconda will increase about 500 times in weight – more than any other snake species.

The blue whale is the biggest animal ever to have lived on our planet – twice the size of the largest dinosaur. This gigantic creature spends all its life in the sea feeding on tiny shrimp-like animals called krill, which it filters from the water. It may eat 3.5 tonnes – about 40 million – of these in a day. Even a newborn baby blue whale is huge, weighing more than a full-grown hippo. It drinks 400 litres of its mother's milk every day – that's about two big bathtubs full!

BIGGEST OF ALL

CRASH...

A blue whale prepares to dive, raising its huge tail, measuring 7.5 m across, above the water. The whale can dive down to 500 m.

SPECIAL FEATURES

HEART: The blue whale's heart weighs as much as a small car – it has to be big to pump blood through the whale's massive body.

BALEEN PLATES: The whale filters food through plates of fringed material called baleen hanging from its upper jaws.

AWESOME...

A mighty blue whale dwarfs this 7-m-long research boat. The whale can swim as fast as an ocean liner, at up to 48 km/h.

Blue whale

Scientific name: *Balaenoptera musculus*
Type: Mammal
Lifespan: 80 years, sometimes 100-plus
Length: 25–32 m
Weight: 180 tonnes, female usually heavier than male
Range: Oceans worldwide
Status: Endangered

STAR FACT

Not only are blue whales the biggest of all animals, they are also among the loudest. They make a wide range of sounds, which can be heard by other blue whales more than 1500 km away.

TONGUE: The tongue of a blue whale weighs at least 2.7 tonnes – as much as an elephant. The whale uses it to push water out of its mouth and krill down its throat.

STREAMLINED BODY: The whale's sleek, tapering shape helps it to move through the water gracefully at high speed.

The biggest of its kind, the giant anteater is a large, powerful animal – but its prey is surprisingly tiny. It eats only ants and termites, tearing open their nests with its strong front feet. The anteater won't destroy the nests completely or kill all the termites because it knows that if it allows the insects to repair their home, it will be able to come back again and again for more meals. Although not an aggressive animal, the giant anteater can wound an attacker with its long claws.

TERMITE TASTER

GREEDY...

An anteater needs a lot of termites or ants to make a meal. It eats as many as 30,000 of these little insects every day!

NOSE AND EARS: The giant anteater tracks down insect nests with the help of its keen sense of smell and good hearing. Its eyesight is poor.

STRONG STOMACH: This mammal has a strong stomach and special digestive juices to break down the tough little creatures it feeds on.

Giant anteater

Scientific name: *Myrmecophaga tridactyla*
Type: Mammal
Lifespan: About 14 years
Length: Head-body 1–2 m, tail up to 90 cm
Weight: 22–39 kg
Range: Central and South America
Status: Near threatened

WEIRD...

The giant anteater is perfectly adapted for its life as one of the most specialized of all insect eaters, with its slender, tapering snout and long, sharp claws.

STAR FACT

This anteater's tongue is 60 cm in length, and covered in tiny spines and sticky saliva. The anteater can flick its tongue out 160 times every minute to gobble up its scurrying insect prey.

SKIN AND HAIR: Long hair and thick skin help to protect the anteater from the bites of termites and ants as they try to defend their nests.

SHARP CLAWS: The claws on a giant anteater's front feet are up to 10 cm in length and very strong – ideal for tearing open termite nests.

The enormous Galapagos tortoise weighs more than four adult humans. It is one of the world's largest tortoises, and one of the biggest of all reptiles. Its massive shell is made of bone, and it can draw its soft head and limbs in underneath it to protect itself. A peaceful and slow-moving creature, the Galapagos tortoise spends a few hours every morning basking in the sunshine to warm itself up and then rambles around feeding on grass, leaves and flowers. It sleeps for at least 14 hours at night.

STAR FACT

This giant is friendly with finches. The birds pick off and eat ticks from the tortoise's folds of skin. The bird gets a meal and the tortoise gets a break from the itchy parasites.

BONY SHELL

LAZY BATHERS...

Galapagos tortoises like water and will bask and even sleep in muddy pools and puddles.

SPECIAL FEATURES

WATER STORES: This tortoise can survive for a year without food or drink, thanks to its very slow systems and its ability to store water in its body.

SENSE OF SMELL: Like other land tortoises, the Galapagos tortoise has a good sense of smell which helps it track down plants to eat.

Galapagos giant tortoise

Scientific name: *Geochelone elephantopus*
Type: Reptile
Lifespan: 100–150 years
Length: Up to 1.2 m
Weight: 300 kg
Range: Galapagos Islands
Status: Vulnerable

YUMMY...

Tortoises that feed on the ground have domed shells, but those that stretch up to feed on higher plants have shells that curve in at the front so that they can lift their heads.

MY STAR RATING

SERRATED JAWS: The lower jaws have tough ridges with serrated (saw-like) edges. These allow the tortoise to bite through cactus stems and other tough plants.

LEGS AND FEET: Short, thick legs shaped like pillars support the Galapagos tortoise's great weight. Its feet are equipped with strong claws to help it dig.

The largest of all spiders, this creepy-crawly has a chunky body and four pairs of long hairy legs. Despite its name, it doesn't usually eat birds, but hunts large insects, lizards and even mice, killing them by biting with its poisonous fangs. Usually active at night, it spends its days sheltering in a silk-lined burrow dug into the ground or under leaves on the forest floor. The female is bigger than the male and will sometimes eat her partner after mating.

HAIRY HORROR

Goliath bird-eating spider

Scientific name: *Theraphosa blondi*
Type: Arachnid
Lifespan: Males 3–6 years, females 10–12 years
Legspan: 30 cm
Weight: 170 g
Range: Northern South America
Status: Not enough information

POUNCE...

This spider is a stealth hunter, pouncing on victims and paralyzing them with its venomous bite, then breaking their flesh down with special digestive juices.

MY STAR RATING

STAR FACT

If disturbed, this spider can make a loud hissing sound by rubbing the bristles on its legs together to warn off the enemy. This sound can be heard more than 4 m away.

SPECIAL FEATURES

FANGS: This spider's fangs are 2.5 cm in length and linked to poison glands. A bite is not fatal for humans but is very painful.

HAIRS: The body is covered with tiny hairs that the spider can flick off at an attacker. These can cause swelling and irritation.

SUPER STINGER

The world's largest wasp, the Japanese giant hornet is a dangerous and aggressive insect. It preys on other insects and can kill a whole colony of bees in just a few hours. The hornets don't actually eat the bees – they chew them up to feed to their larvae. The adult hornets then drink a saliva made by the larvae that is said to provide them with amazing energy. They can fly nearly 100 kilometres in a day at speeds of up to 40 kilometres an hour.

STRIKE...

This hornet can kill 40 honeybees in a minute. In Japan it kills more people every year than any other animal, including snakes.

Japanese giant hornet

Scientific name: *Vespa mandarinia*
Type: Insect
Lifespan: Probably several months
Length: 5 cm
Wingspan: Up to 7.5 cm
Range: Eastern Asia
Status: Least concern

MY STAR RATING

STAR FACT

In Japan, they make a drink called hornet juice based on the saliva made by hornet larvae. This miracle drink is said to boost the performance of athletes.

SPECIAL FEATURES

STING: The hornet has a 6 mm sting that it drives into its prey to inject its venom, and which can be used over and over again.

VENOM: The giant hornet's venom contains a chemical substance strong enough to dissolve human tissue.

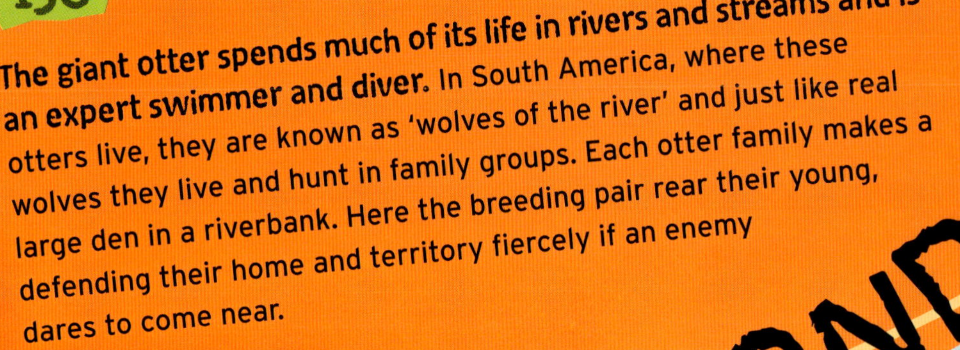

The giant otter spends much of its life in rivers and streams and is an expert swimmer and diver. In South America, where these otters live, they are known as 'wolves of the river' and just like real wolves they live and hunt in family groups. Each otter family makes a large den in a riverbank. Here the breeding pair rear their young, defending their home and territory fiercely if an enemy dares to come near.

WEBBED WONDER

TASTY...

Fish, such as piranhas, are this predator's main food and the otter may eat several kilograms of fish every day. It also catches crabs and even snakes.

THICK FUR: The giant otter's very thick, dense fur is water repellent, helping to keep the animal warm and dry.

FEET AND TAIL: Large webbed feet and a long, very muscular tail help make the otter an agile, powerful swimmer.

STAR FACT

Most of the otter's fur is reddish brown, but it has a patch of creamy fur on its throat. Its shape is different in every otter, so people can recognize individuals from their markings.

Giant otter

Scientific name: *Pteroneura brasiliensis*
Type: Mammal
Lifespan: 8–10 years
Length: Head-body 1–1.4 m, tail up to 65 cm
Weight: Males up to 34 kg, females up to 26 kg
Range: Northern South America
Status: Endangered

GETTING AROUND...

The giant otter moves more awkwardly on land than in water, but still manages to travel long distances between rivers and lakes.

SPECIAL EARS: The giant otter is able to close off its ears when it dives for food to prevent water from getting inside them.

WHISKERS: The long whiskers are highly sensitive to touch, helping the otter to find prey in muddy or sandy water where visibility is poor.

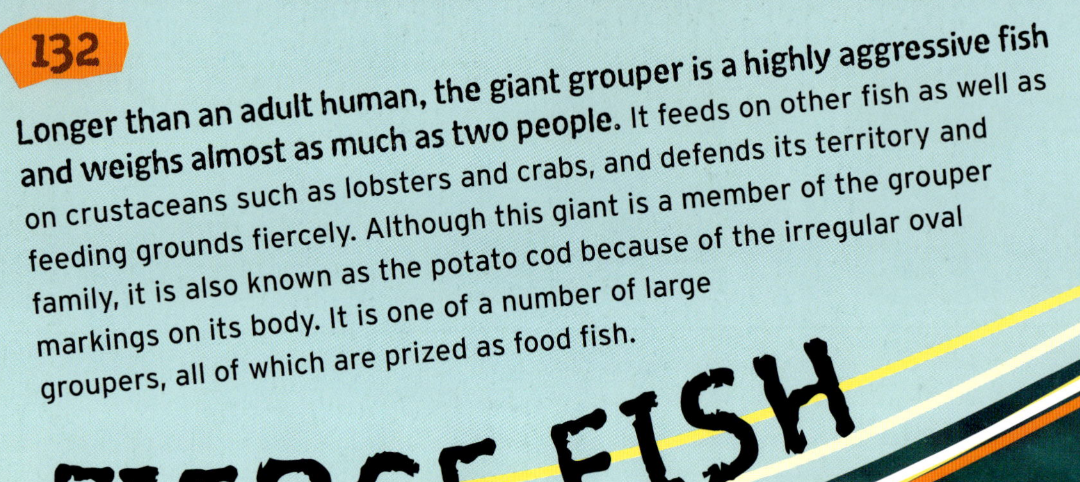

Longer than an adult human, the giant grouper is a highly aggressive fish and weighs almost as much as two people. It feeds on other fish as well as on crustaceans such as lobsters and crabs, and defends its territory and feeding grounds fiercely. Although this giant is a member of the grouper family, it is also known as the potato cod because of the irregular oval markings on its body. It is one of a number of large groupers, all of which are prized as food fish.

FIERCE FISH

SURPRISE...

The giant grouper lives around coral reefs where it is usually the largest of the inhabitants. It hides among the coral and ambushes any prey that swims past.

STAR FACT

Most groupers start life as females, and become male when they have grown to about 12 kg in weight. If there are no males in an area, a female becomes male sooner.

BIG MOUTH: Like all groupers, this fish has a very large mouth than can engulf any unwary prey that comes within range.

SHARP TEETH: Some of the teeth at the front of the jaw face inwards, making it tricky for prey to escape once they are inside the grouper's mouth.

Giant grouper

Scientific name: *Epinephelus tukula*
Type: Fish
Lifespan: Up to 50 years
Length: Up to 2 m
Weight: 110 kg
Range: Tropical and subtropical waters of the Indian Ocean and western Pacific Ocean
Status: Least concern

BACK OFF...

Giant groupers are inquisitive fish and often swim up to investigate divers. However it's best not to get too close, as they can be dangerous.

MY STAR RATING

CAMOUFLAGE: The irregular dark markings on the grouper's body help it to stay hidden among the rocks and coral as it lies in wait for unwary prey.

COLOUR CHANGE: Groupers can change colour from dark to light to match their surroundings and make their camouflage even more effective.

The huge, bulky-bodied hippopotamus spends most of its time wallowing in lakes or rivers to keep cool. Despite its less-than-agile build it is a surprisingly good swimmer, but it's so big that it can often walk along the river or lake bed rather than swim. At night, hippos haul themselves out of the water onto land where they feed on massive quantities of grass. They live in groups of about 15 or so females and young, led by an adult male, but may sometimes gather in large herds of up to 150 animals.

BARREL BODY

AAHH...

A newborn hippo weighs up to 50 kg – more than an average 12-year-old child. It swims before it can walk and feeds on its mother's milk underwater.

SPECIAL FEATURES

NATURAL MOISTURE: The hippo's thick skin contains an oily substance. This acts like a natural sunblock, and prevents the skin from cracking.

EYES AND NOSE: Nostrils and eyes are set high on the hippo's head so it can see and breathe when lying almost submerged in water.

Hippopotamus

Scientific name: *Hippopotamus amphibius*
Type: Mammal
Lifespan: Up to 40 years
Length: Head-body up to 5 m, tail 50 cm
Weight: Up to 4.5 tonnes
Range: Parts of Africa south of the Sahara
Status: Vulnerable

SCENT MARKING: Hippos mark their territory by leaving heaps of dung on the river bank and may even spread it around with their tails to warn off enemies.

MOUTH AND TEETH: The mouth measures up to 1.2 m across. The lower canine teeth are 30 cm long and weigh as much as 3 kg – equal to three bags of sugar.

DEADLY LIZARD

The largest, heaviest lizard on Earth, the Komodo dragon looks like a creature that belongs to the age of dinosaurs. This fierce predator is armed with sharp claws and large, jagged teeth, and will eat almost anything it can catch, from deer and pigs to much larger animals such as water buffalo. Very little is wasted and the dragons will even eat bones, hooves and skin. They will also scavenge carrion (animals that are already dead). Like many reptiles, Komodos reproduce by laying eggs.

GROSS...

Komodos eat up to 80 percent of their own body weight in a single meal, and will happily feast on dead marine animals such as dolphins that wash up on the shore of their island home.

SPECIAL FEATURES

TONGUE: The dragon's tongue flicks in and out constantly, analyzing the air for the scent of prey. It can detect a dead animal from over 8 km away.

TEETH: A Komodo dragon has more than 60 teeth, each up to 2.5 cm in length. The teeth have serrated edges like those of sharks.

LOOK OUT...

Despite its bulky shape and short stocky legs, the Komodo is a fast mover and can run at speeds of up to 18 km/h over short distances as it chases its prey. It is also a good swimmer.

Komodo dragon

Scientific name: *Varanus komodoensis*
Type: Reptile
Lifespan: About 30 years
Length: 3 m
Weight: 150 kg
Range: Lesser Sunda Islands, Indonesia
Status: Vulnerable

STAR FACT

Venom glands in the Komodo's jaws mean that if it bites a victim that then escapes, the dragon just has to follow its prey and wait. In 24 hours the wounded animal will die from the effects of the poison.

MY STAR RATING

FLEXIBLE JAWS: To enable it to tear off and swallow large pieces of flesh, the Komodo has a huge mouth and powerful, flexible jaws.

TAIL: The dragon's tail is as long as its body and very heavy. It can use it as a support when standing up on its hind legs to reach prey.

TERRIBLE TENTACLES

Can you imagine a jellyfish with a body bigger than a double bed and trailing tentacles longer than a bus? That is about the size of the lion's mane jellyfish, the largest known of its kind. This amazing creature gets its name from its mass of thin, hairlike tentacles, which it uses for capturing prey such as small fish and shellfish. They are most common in cold waters and the biggest specimens are found in the Arctic Ocean.

STAR FACT

A jellyfish's body actually consists of around 95 percent water, and although they are animals, they have no bones, blood or brain!

WHOA...

The biggest ever lion's mane jellyfish is said to have had tentacles longer than a blue whale, the largest animal in the world.

SPECIAL FEATURES

STINGING CELLS: The jellyfish's super-long tentacles are lined with stinging cells that release barbed stingers upon contact, paralyzing prey.

BELL: A jellyfish's saucer-shaped body is called a bell, and its mouth is located at the centre of the underside of the bell.

Lion's mane jellyfish

Scientific name: *Cyanea capillata*
Type: Cnidarian
Lifespan: About 1 year
Length: Bell up to 2 m across, tentacles 30 m-plus
Weight: 200 kg
Range: Arctic and cooler waters of Atlantic and Pacific oceans
Status: Not enough information

The jellyfish's stinging cells can be very dangerous to humans and cause painful wounds so if you see one, stay well clear!

DON'T TOUCH...

TENTACLES: The extraordinarily long tentacles of this jellyfish are grouped in eight clusters, with each cluster containing about 150 tentacles.

ORAL ARMS: As well as its tentacles, the lion's mane jellyfish also has special arms called oral arms for carrying food to its mouth.

The largest of all land crabs, the spectacular coconut crab is a kind of hermit crab, so it does not have a hard shell. A young coconut crab shelters in a discarded snail shell, but when it gets too big for this it grows a tough, protective skin over its body. This crab is so well adapted to life on land that it has lost the ability to swim. Coconuts are its main food, but it also eats other fruits and leaves and will gobble up the discarded shells of other crustaceans.

MEGA PINCERS

Giant coconut crab

Scientific name: Birgus latro
Type: Crustacean
Lifespan: Up to 40 years
Legspan: 1 m
Weight: 3 kg
Range: Islands in the Indian and Pacific oceans
Status: Not enough information

STAR FACT

This giant crab is so strong that it can lift objects such as rocks or branches that weigh as much as 28 kg – the weight of an average eight- or nine-year-old child!

SCUTTLE...

These crabs climb coconut palms with ease and are able to open coconut shells with their huge claws to get at the flesh inside.

MY STAR RATING

SPECIAL FEATURES

TEN LEGS: This crab has five pairs of legs. The front pair is not used for walking and bears huge claws for breaking open its food.

SENSE OF SMELL: Coconut crabs are able to pick up the scent of food such as coconuts and bananas over long distances.

HEAVY HULK

The bison, also known as the American buffalo, is the largest, heaviest land animal in North America. This impressive beast has a massive head, bulky shoulders and shaggy fur. Males and females generally live in separate herds, roaming the plains and feeding on grasses and shrubs. They come together in the mating season when rival males may battle with one another for the right to mate with females.

ZOOM...

Despite their size, bison are surprisingly fast runners, speeding along at up to 65 km/h to escape predators such as wolves.

STAR FACT

There were millions of bison in North America, but in the late 19th century they were hunted nearly to extinction. Now the numbers are rising again and there are about 200,000.

Bison

Scientific name: *Bison bison*
Type: Mammal
Lifespan: 12–20 years
Length: Head-body up to 3.5 m, tail 60 cm
Weight: Up to 1000 kg
Range: North America
Status: Near threatened

MY STAR RATING

SPECIAL FEATURES

THICK COAT: The bison's long and shaggy coat keeps it warm during the harsh winters on the prairie. It sheds some hair in spring.

HORNS: The huge horns are up to 61 cm in length. They are made of bone and covered with keratin – the same substance as human fingernails.

A huge male gorilla, standing upright and making blood-curdling roaring sounds, is a fearsome sight. In fact the gorilla is usually a peaceful animal, and feeds mostly on plants, but the male will fight to the death to protect his family. When angered, gorillas will roar, pound their chests, then charge towards the enemy if necessary. Gorillas are the biggest and strongest of all the primates and the male is about twice the size of a female.

GENTLE GIANT

AAHHH...

Adult gorillas might be giants, but a baby gorilla weighs only about 2 kg at birth – much less than an average human baby. It feeds on mum's milk for about a year and stays close to her for at least three years.

SPECIAL FEATURES

BIG AND STRONG: A male gorilla is at least twice the weight of the average human man and more than four times as strong.

NOSE PRINT: Each gorilla has a slightly different pattern of wrinkles and folds on its nose. Gorillas can be identified by their nose prints.

Mountain gorilla

Scientific name: *Gorilla beringei beringei*
Type: Mammal
Lifespan: About 35 years in the wild
Height: Up to 1.8 m (males); 1.5 m (females)
Weight: Up to 210 kg (males); 115 kg (females)
Range: Virunga mountains in Rwanda, Uganda and the Democratic Republic of Congo
Status: Endangered

STAY AWAY...

A gorilla family is led by a full-grown male and includes some younger males, females and their young. The leading male is called a silverback because he has silvery hair on his back and shoulders.

LONG ARMS: Gorillas can stand upright but usually walk on all fours. Their arms are longer than their legs and span about 2.5 m when outstretched.

SUPER CLIMBER: Despite their size, gorillas are agile animals and even big males can climb trees to find food and make sleeping nests.

The majestic wandering albatross has the largest wingspan of any bird. From tip to tip the wings measure an amazing 3.4 metres – as much as a small car. The albatross spends most of its life in flight, gliding on air currents over the sea. The wind does most of the work, so the bird hardly needs to beat its massive wings. It lands on the sea only to feed and usually just dips its head and beak below the surface to snatch fish or squid.

HIGH FLIER

SQUAWK...

This albatross rarely comes to land except to breed. The female lays only one egg and the parents care for their chick for about nine months.

SPECIAL FEATURES

HOOKED BEAK: The strong beak, with its sharp edges and hooked tip, is ideally shaped for catching slippery fish and tearing them apart.

SENSE OF SMELL: Unlike many birds, albatrosses have a good sense of smell, and can scent floating carrion from several kilometres away.

Wandering albatross

Scientific name: *Diomedea exulans*
Type: Bird
Lifespan: 30 years
Length: 1.1 m
Weight: 8–11.5 kg
Range: Southern oceans
Status: Vulnerable

STAR FACT

Albatrosses are capable of flying huge distances. One bird was tracked travelling 6000 km over the course of only 12 days – that's 500 km every day.

FOLLOW THAT FOOD...

Albatrosses often follow fishing boats, swooping down to feed on the scraps that get thrown overboard.

MY STAR RATING

WEBBED FEET: The albatross uses its large webbed feet for paddling when on the water's surface and as brakes when in flight.

SALT GLANDS: Special glands near the eyes help remove the salt that builds up in the albatross' body from its prey and sea water.

ARMOURED HUNTER

At least twice the length of an adult human, the saltwater crocodile is the biggest of all croc species. It is a fierce predator and lurks in shallow water where it watches and waits for prey. If a potential victim such as a buffalo, monkey or wild boar ventures near the water's edge, the crocodile lunges with surprising speed and seizes the animal in its huge jaws. It then drags its catch back to the water and pulls it under the surface. Once the creature has drowned, the saltie can feed, biting off large chunks of flesh.

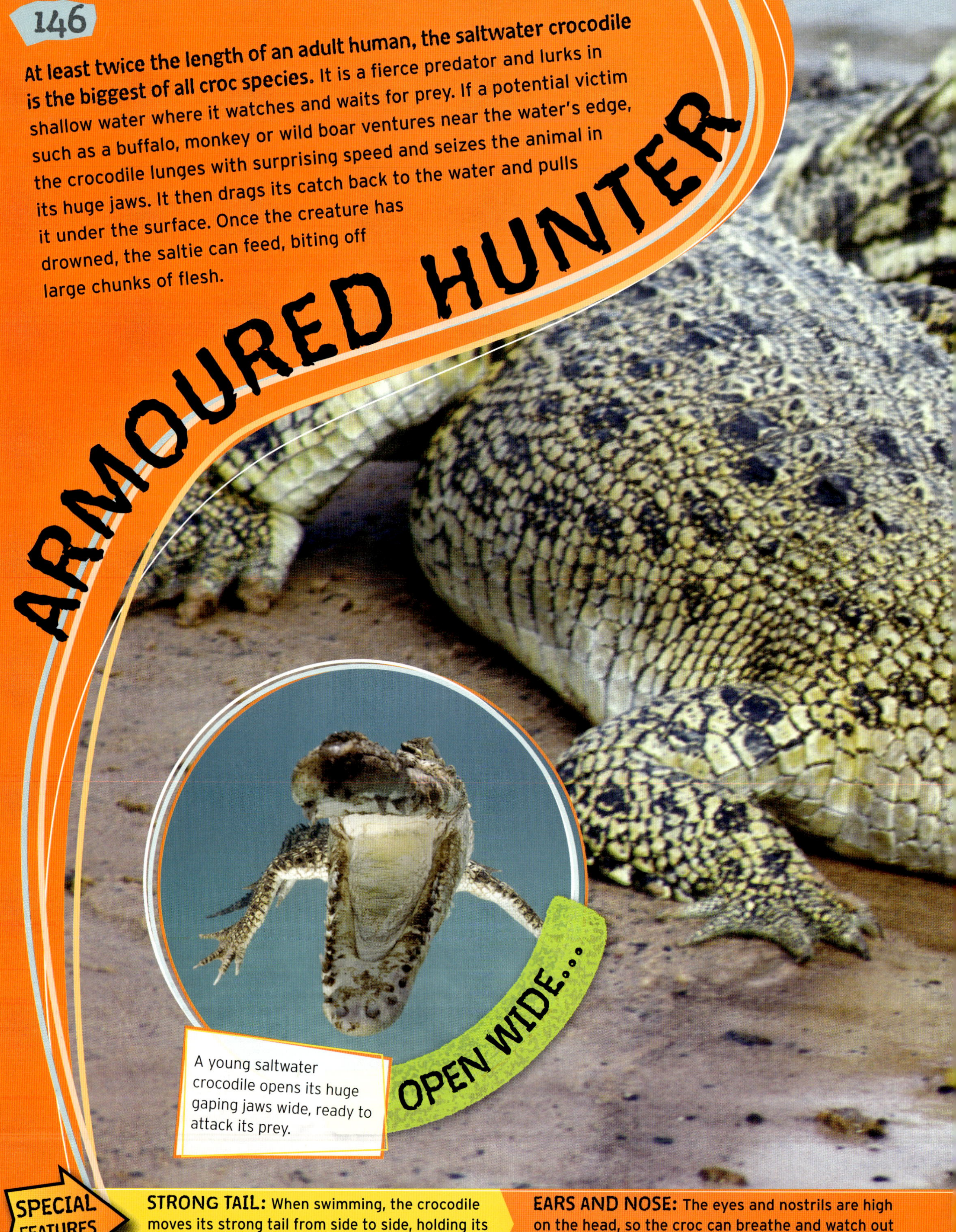

OPEN WIDE...

A young saltwater crocodile opens its huge gaping jaws wide, ready to attack its prey.

SPECIAL FEATURES

STRONG TAIL: When swimming, the crocodile moves its strong tail from side to side, holding its legs close to its sides.

EARS AND NOSE: The eyes and nostrils are high on the head, so the croc can breathe and watch out for prey while lying almost submerged in water.

MOVE IT...

On land the crocodile can wriggle along on its tummy, pushing with its feet, or lift itself up off the ground to move more rapidly.

Saltwater crocodile

Scientific name: *Crocodylus porosus*
Type: Reptile
Lifespan: About 70 years
Length: 6 m
Weight: 450 kg
Range: Southeast Asia, northern Australia
Status: Least concern

STAR FACT

Female crocs lay eggs in nests made from mounds of plant matter and mud. If the nest temperature is about 31.5°C the hatchlings will be males. If it is warmer or cooler they will be females.

TEETH: The crocodile's long, powerful jaws house up to 68 sharp teeth, which help it to quickly tear even large prey into chunks small enough to swallow.

BODY ARMOUR: Embedded in the thick skin on the crocodile's back are pieces of bone that help to protect it from the bites and scratches of struggling prey.

Like a huge underwater bird, the manta ray moves through the surface waters of the ocean by flapping its enormous winglike fins. Although it is the largest of the rays and a close relative of sharks it is not a fierce hunter, instead feeding on small planktonic creatures (microscopic animals and plants), which it filters from the water through special spongy plates on its gills. A manta ray may eat more than 17 kilograms of its tiny prey every day.

WINGED SWIMMER

GULP...

The ray uses the long lobes on either side of its head to funnel water into its mouth. Small fish and plankton become trapped on the manta's gill plates while the water flows out again.

CARTILAGE: Like other rays and sharks, the manta's skeleton is made of cartilage (a tough, gristly material), making its 'wings' very flexible.

SPECIAL HELPERS: Small fish such as wrasse help mantas by removing parasites and cleaning any wounds on their bodies.

Manta ray

Scientific name: *Manta birostris*
Type: Fish
Lifespan: About 20 years
Width: Up to 7 m
Weight: Up to 1.3 tonnes
Range: Temperate, subtropical and tropical waters worldwide
Status: Near threatened

STAR FACT

The manta ray makes regular migrations (seasonal journeys) across the Indian Ocean. One ray was tracked travelling an incredible 1100 km in just 60 days.

SPLASH...

The manta is a graceful swimmer and will sometimes make spectacular leaps above the water's surface.

MY STAR RATING

TEETH: Inside its huge, cavernous mouth the manta has 18 rows of small teeth on its lower jaw, but these are not used for trapping food.

COLOURATION: The underside of the body is pale with dark blotches. The pattern is different in every manta and can be used to identify individuals.

SUPER SLITHERER

This monster mollusc is the world's largest land snail. It comes from East Africa and has now spread to many other tropical areas. A big eater, it chomps its way through large amounts of almost any plants it can find – including food crops, so it is generally considered to be a pest. Like many snails, this giant is usually active at night and spends its days buried in damp earth. It stays underground during long dry periods too, until rain tempts it out into the open air again.

WOW...

On the snail's head are two sets of tentacles. The longer pair carry its eyes and the shorter set help the snail to touch and smell.

STAR FACT

In 1966 an American boy brought three of these snails back from Hawaii to Florida, USA and let them loose in his garden. Seven years later there were more than 18,000 of these snails in the state.

TAKE ME HOME...

This snail is as big as an adult human's hand. Some people like them so much that they keep them as pets.

SPECIAL FEATURES

SHELL: Like all snails, this giant can pull its vulnerable soft body into its hard outer shell to protect itself from predators.

SLIME: The snail moves along on its large flattened body, called a foot. The foot gives off slime, which helps the snail to slither along.

Giant African land snail

Scientific name: *Achatina fulica*
Type: Mollusc
Lifespan: Up to 9 years
Length: Shell up to 20 cm, extended body up to 30 cm
Weight: Up to 450 g
Range: East Africa, but has been introduced to many other tropical areas
Status: Least concern

ROUGH TONGUE: A tongue-like structure covered with lots of tiny toothlike spikes helps the snail scrape up its food.

FAST BREEDER: This snail lays five or six batches of as many as 200 eggs each year. Most of the babies survive so the species spreads fast.

The world's largest octopus spends its time lurking among rocks below the water's surface. Concealed in the murky shadows it watches for prey such as crabs and scallops, which it then pulls apart with its strong, sucker-lined arms. The arms are linked to a rounded structure called the mantle, which is actually its head and body combined. Octopuses are thought to be the most intelligent of all invertebrates (animals without backbones).

ARMED AND READY

Pacific giant octopus

Scientific name: *Octopus dofleini*
Type: Mollusc
Lifespan: About 4 years
Length: 5 m
Weight: 40 kg on average but largest recorded was 272 kg
Range: Pacific coast of North America
Status: Not assessed

WHOOSH...

Like all octopuses, this giant swims by jet propulsion. It sucks water into the web of skin at the base of its arms then quickly expels it to push itself forwards at speed.

STAR FACT

When resting, the octopus' colour matches its surroundings. But when angry or alarmed it can change to brighter colours to warn off enemies or scare away rivals.

MY STAR RATING

SPECIAL FEATURES

EIGHT ARMS: The arms are lined with two rows of suction cups. There are about 260 cups on each arm, which help the octopus hold onto prey.

EYES: An octopus has very large eyes and excellent eyesight. Its eyes are very similar in structure to human eyes.

SHARKS

ULTIMATE KILLERS

Sharks are super predators. Fast and fierce, they can detect prey over great distances. They race in and bite with great power, their razor teeth slicing through flesh, gristle and bone.

Not all sharks are so deadly. The largest of the 400-plus kinds are as big as a bus, yet these giants spend their time filtering tiny planktonic creatures from the sea water. Even the most fearsome predatory sharks rarely attack humans. Road accidents and wasp stings kill more people than shark attacks.

LAZY BATHER

Its habit of lazily cruising through the water, sometimes rolling onto its side as though soaking up the sunshine, gave the basking shark its name. This giant – the world's second-largest fish – is far from fierce. As it swims through a shoal of plankton (microscopic creatures that drift in ocean currents), its gaping mouth is one metre wide and one metre high. Water passes into the mouth and out through the gaps between the frilly gill rakers on the sides of the head. Plankton sticks to the rakers and is then sucked down into the shark's stomach.

WE CAN SEE YOU...

The basking shark's tall, triangular fin often pokes above the water's surface as it feeds.

STAR FACT

Up to one-quarter of a basking shark's weight is its massive liver. This stores food and also contains vast amounts of oils, which are lighter than water and help the shark to float.

SPECIAL FEATURES

SPEED: A basking shark usually swims at a speed slightly slower than we walk. But it can also surge at high speed and even leap clear of the water.

FINS: Its massive front pair of fins (pectorals), give a huge area for control in the water, so this shark can twist and turn surprisingly fast.

Basking shark

Scientific name: *Cetorhinus maximus*
Shark group: Cetorhinidae
Lifespan: Probably 50-plus years
Length: 8–10 m, rarely exceeds 12 m
Weight: Up to 6 tonnes
Range: Oceans worldwide
Status: Vulnerable

RAKERS: The plankton-sieving gill rakers nearly join at the top and bottom, forming an almost complete circle around the shark's head.

JAWS: No other shark can gape at such a wide angle as the basking shark, which swims along with its bendy top and bottom jaws stretched to their limit.

UNDERWATER WOLVES

Blue sharks have a habit of following fishing boats in packs, feeding hungrily on discarded scraps thrown overboard. When whaling (whale hunting) was common, they were known for tearing apart whales that were being towed by whaling ships, so sailors called them 'wolves of the sea'. Slim, sleek and speedy, the blue shark can dart and dodge as it chases many kinds of prey, such as fish, squid, crabs and even young dolphins or porpoises.

ATTACK...

Once one blue shark in the group begins to attack a shoal of fish, the others quickly follow, in the typical shark 'feeding frenzy'.

SPECIAL FEATURES

SHAPE: Its cone-shaped nose and streamlined body mean that the blue shark can swim thousands of kilometres without much effort.

LONG FINS: Very long pectoral fins produce an upward force that helps the shark avoid sinking as it cruises along.

Blue shark

Scientific name: *Prionace glauca*
Shark group: Carcharhinidae
Lifespan: Probably 20-plus years
Length: 3–3.5 m, occasionally 4 m
Weight: 150 kg, rarely 250 kg
Range: Worldwide tropical to cool oceans
Status: Near threatened

STAR FACT

The blue is the shark world's greatest traveller. It regularly swims across whole oceans such as the Pacific or Atlantic on its endless hunt for food, and also as part of its breeding cycle.

DINNER TIME...

Blue sharks form a pack as they circle a shoal of small fish, such as these anchovies, driving them into a tight 'bait ball'. Then the sharks dash in one by one to eat their prey.

MY STAR RATING

SKIN: Shark skin has thousands of tiny pointed 'teeth' called placoid scales or denticles. These allow water to slip past very smoothly, making swimming easier.

VISION: Most sharks have reasonable eyesight for close objects, and the blue shark's large, dark eyes are good for distance vision too.

Most animals never know that a great white is approaching until the world's biggest hunting fish crashes into them. Also known as the white pointer, blue pointer or simply 'man-eater', this predator usually surges up at its prey from dim water below and makes one fast, smash-and-grab bite. Then it backs off to taste the bits of flesh and blood in its mouth, and waits for its victim to weaken. If the shark likes its first mouthful, then it really gets to work, tearing off great chunks to swallow.

WHITE DEATH

SLICE...

The great white bite has awesome power, much greater even than that of wolves. It slices easily through gristle and even bone.

SPECIAL FEATURES

WARM BLOOD: This shark can raise its body temperature 10°C above the surrounding water, allowing it to swim faster than other, colder fish.

JAWS: Like all sharks, a great white's skeleton is made of flexible cartilage, not bone. So its jaws can bend to soak up the sudden impact of its attack.

As this great white clamps its jaws onto a seal, the power of its rapid attack causes it to leap clear of the water and 'low-fly' for several metres.

Great white shark

Scientific name: *Carcharodon carcharias*
Shark group: Lamnidae
Lifespan: 20–30 years, rarely 50-plus
Length: Up to 7 m (females larger)
Weight: Up to 2 tonnes
Range: All warm and temperate seas
Status: Endangered

STAR FACT

The great white 'spy-hops' (holds its body upright and pokes its head above the surface), presumably to look around. This is unusual among sharks but common in whales and dolphins.

TEETH: In the upper jaw, the teeth are triangular, blade-like and saw-edged for cutting. Teeth in the lower jaw are thinner and pointed for stabbing and holding.

SAW-BITE: For a big meal such as a whale, the great white bites deep and then shakes its head from side to side, to saw and cut off lumps.

The great white may be the biggest predatory fish, but the Greenland shark comes a close second. This massive monster usually lives in deep, cold water and rarely rushes anywhere. One of its favourite feasts is a 'whale fall' – a huge whale that has died and sunk to the sea bed. The Greenland shark will spend days biting and gnawing meat from the rotting carcass. When it has finally eaten its fill, it will be half as heavy again as when it arrived.

SCARY SCAVENGER

The Greenland shark is also called the sleeper shark because it moves so slowly and will sometimes hang motionless in the water, as though it has gone to sleep.

SPECIAL FEATURES

SPEED: Although it usually swims slowly, the Greenland shark can swish its huge tail for a burst of speed if needed, such as when hunting salmon.

SENSES: Parasites living inside the eyes of some Greenland sharks cause blindness, but the sharks can still use their senses of smell and touch to find food.

Greenland shark

Scientific name: *Somniosus microcephalus*
Shark group: Somniosidael
Lifespan: Unknown, possibly 100 years
Length: Up to 7 m (female larger)
Weight: Rarely over 1.2 tonnes
Range: Atlantic and Arctic oceans
Status: Near threatened

HI THERE...

This Greenland shark has swum into the shallow, lighter water of a river estuary. Lucky divers who spot it can get better photographs here than in the dark deep.

STAR FACT

The stomach contents of dead Greenland sharks show that they eat other sharks, salmon, many kinds of whales and dolphins, caribou (reindeer), and once even a polar bear!

MY STAR RATING

DEEP DIVING: This shark can dive down to 2000 m or more, where few other big fish go, to feed on sunken dead bodies of all kinds.

TEETH: The 100 or so teeth are quite small, suited to a wide range of foods. They are narrow in the upper jaw and wide in the lower one.

FRESHLY KILLED

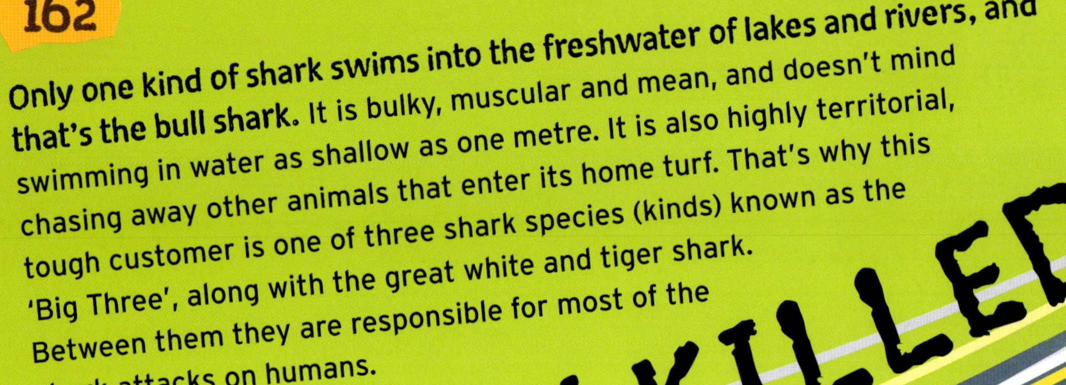

Only one kind of shark swims into the freshwater of lakes and rivers, and that's the bull shark. It is bulky, muscular and mean, and doesn't mind swimming in water as shallow as one metre. It is also highly territorial, chasing away other animals that enter its home turf. That's why this tough customer is one of three shark species (kinds) known as the 'Big Three', along with the great white and tiger shark. Between them they are responsible for most of the shark attacks on humans.

HUNGRY...

The bull shark will take a bite out of almost any creature, from smaller animals such as seabirds and turtles, to other sharks and even humans.

SPECIAL FEATURES

FEMALE SIZE: A female bull shark can be twice as long and three times heavier than a male. He must be wary – she could eat him!

HABITAT: Although they can swim in freshwater, thanks to some unusual body features, bull sharks are thought to return to saltwater to breed.

Bull shark

Scientific name: *Carcharhinus leucas*
Shark group: Carcharhinidae
Lifespan: 20–25 years
Length: Male 2.5 m, female 4 m
Weight: Male 120 kg, female 300 kg
Range: Warm coastal waters, rivers and lakes
Status: Near threatened

LET'S BE FRIENDS...

In the late summer bull sharks gather in groups to breed. For the rest of the year they prowl alone, although sometimes two of them form a 'friendship' and hunt together.

STAR FACT

Bull shark attacks on humans have been recorded at locations more than 2000 km from the ocean. They have been known to bite people who have come to a riverbank to wash their clothes or swim.

AGGRESSION: Bull sharks are unpredictable – peaceful one moment, then aggressive and dangerous the next. As a result, few other animals trouble them.

BUMPING: Before racing in to bite, a bull shark will often nudge or bump a potential victim with its nose, to see how it reacts.

Not all sharks are huge, bloodthirsty predators. Some are fairly small – but they can still be deadly. Many are known as dogfish or houndfish, as they hunt shoals of fish in packs. They have two dorsal (back) fins, each with a sharp spur (spine) at the front, so they are also known as spurdogs. The spines are sharp, and can inject venom into an attacker. The poison causes a painful throbbing ache in humans and also in the shark's predators, which quickly learn to leave it alone.

SNEAK ATTACK

Spiny dogfish

Scientific name: *Squalus acanthias*
Shark group: Squalidae
Lifespan: 35-plus years
Length: Up to 1 m
Weight: Up to 7 kg
Range: Cool to temperate Pacific and western Atlantic oceans
Status: Vulnerable

STAR FACT

Few other sharks have as many common names as the spiny dogfish – spiked dogfish, spiny spurdog, piked dogfish, common spurdog, piked spurshark, cape shark and cape dogfish are just a few!

LURK...

Dogfish lurk close to the sea bed, watching for any kind of prey from small fish to crabs, shellfish, prawns and even sea anemones.

SPECIAL FEATURES

COUNTER-SHADING: As in many other species, the shark's dark back blends with the sea bed, while its pale belly matches the lighter water above.

BABIES: Female spiny dogfish are pregnant for the same amount of time as female elephants. Pups are born 22 months after they start to develop.

FLAT FISH

The angel shark lies quite still on the sea bed. It has flicked sand and pebbles over itself to hide the outline of its wide, flat body, so it merges almost perfectly with its surroundings. It watches and waits until it senses a suitable fish swimming past just above. Then with frightening speed the angel shark lurches up and grabs the victim with its many small, sharp teeth. It is an ambush predator – long periods of waiting, then sudden deadly action.

HIDE...

The angel shark tries to bury itself so that only its nostrils, eyes and the breathing openings near them (the spiracles) are exposed.

Pacific angel shark

Scientific name: *Squatina californica*
Shark group: Squatinidae
Lifespan: Unknown, probably 20 years
Length: Up to 1.5 m
Weight: Up to 30 kg
Range: Pacific coasts of the Americas
Status: Near threatened

STAR FACT

This shark's side fins (two pectorals and two pelvics), are very flat and stick out sideways. They look almost like the wings of an aircraft – or of an angel, giving the shark its common name.

MY STAR RATING

SPECIAL FEATURES

WIDE MOUTH: The strong mouth can protrude (extend forwards), stretching to form a wide tube for grabbing prey.

TRAP-JAWS: As the angel shark's mouth encloses the meal, its upper and lower jaws flick shut over it like a spring-loaded trap.

SUPER SENSITIVE

No other fish could be mistaken for the hammerhead shark. Of the nine species, most common is the scalloped hammerhead, named for the scalloped (wave-shaped) front edge of its strange head. It is not known why the eyes and nostrils are set so far apart on the hammer 'lobes', but it may increase the shark's sensitivity to smells floating through the water. Wide-set nostrils mean a smell would be much stronger in one nostril than the other, enabling the hammerhead to locate the source of the smell more quickly.

EYE SPY...

The position of their eyes, out on the ends of the head lobes, gives hammerheads a wider field of view than other sharks, which may help them locate prey faster.

SPECIAL FEATURES

SWINGING: As it swims, the hammerhead swings its head from side to side, perhaps to detect electric signals from animals in the mud.

LATERAL LINE: All sharks have a row of sensors along the side of the body – the lateral line. It detects movement in the water made by other animals.

STAR FACT

Hammerheads regularly hunt stingrays, which hide in mud and sand on the sea bed. They even swallow the ray's hard, dagger-like tail sting. The poison does not seem to affect them.

Scalloped hammerhead shark

Scientific name: *Sphyrna lewini*
Shark group: Sphyrnidae
Lifespan: Unclear, possibly 30 years
Length: 4 m
Weight: 150 kg
Range: Coastal warm to tropical oceans
Status: Endangered

GETTING TOGETHER...

Thousands of hammerheads gather in vast shoals to find partners at breeding time.

MY STAR RATING

HEAD 'WING': Its head is shaped rather like the wing of an aircraft, giving a lifting force as the hammerhead swims, which helps it to avoid sinking.

MOUTH: This shark's mouth is quite small compared to its body size because it specializes in eating fish and squid rather than really big victims.

Named for its yellow-brown upper side and much paler, yellow-tinged underside, the lemon shark is a medium-sized bottom feeder. It eats many kinds of fish, including rays, but it also gobbles up crustaceans such as crabs and crayfish, and even the occasional seabird. Lemon sharks may attack people who come too close, but there are no known human deaths. Sadly it is caught in large numbers and has become less common in recent years.

YELLOW BELLY

GIVING BIRTH...

The mother lemon shark gives birth to between five and 15 babies among the tangled roots of mangrove trees along the shore. The youngsters are about 60 cm in length.

SPECIAL FEATURES

SURVIVAL: Compared to most sharks, lemon sharks survive well in captivity. Studying them helps us to find out more about sharks in general.

LEARNING: Experiments with captive lemon sharks show that they learn quickly and remember tricks even after a gap of six months.

Lemon shark

Scientific name: *Negaprion brevirostris*
Shark group: Carcharhinidae
Lifespan: Unknown, possibly 25 years
Length: 3 m
Weight: 150 kg
Range: Coastal Atlantic and eastern Pacific oceans
Status: Near threatened

STAR FACT

Lemon sharks are among the most saleable of sharks. People eat the flesh, boil the fins into soup, and make the skin into leather goods. They are not rare yet – but they soon could be.

LET'S GO...

Lemon sharks hang around inshore bays, harbours and estuaries during the night, then set off to hunt in deeper offshore waters by day.

MY STAR RATING

DORSAL FINS: The lemon shark has two dorsal fins. The first is typically tall and shark-like but the second is unusually small and far back, just in front of the tail.

TEETH: Its smallish teeth are narrow, sharp and slightly curved, ideal for holding slippery, struggling prey such as fish and squid.

Leopards are spotty, fierce feline predators on land – and leopard sharks are the underwater version. These medium-sized carpet sharks laze around by day, resting on the sea floor, and rarely move unless threatened by a bigger shark. But at night they sneak into action and cruise slowly just above the reef, searching for prey such as smaller fish, squid and shellfish. The leopard shark's tail fin is almost as long as its body and useful for sudden bursts of speed.

WELL SPOTTED!

STAR FACT

Some sharks have spiracles (extra breathing holes just behind the eyes). In the leopard shark the spiracles can be even bigger than the eyes, giving it the nickname 'four-eyed shark'.

SPECIAL FEATURES

SMELL: As in all sharks, scent particles in water float into the leopard shark's nostril chambers where micro-detectors sense them.

EYES: Sharks have an eyelid-like part called the nictitating membrane. This can move over the eye to protect it.

DOTTY...

Each leopard shark has its own pattern of patches and spots, which are different from every other leopard shark.

Leopard shark

Scientific name: *Stegostoma fasciatum*
Shark group: Orectolobiformes
Lifespan: Unknown, possibly 20–25 years
Length: 3 m
Weight: 250 kg
Range: Indian and western Pacific oceans
Status: Vulnerable

GROWING UP...

Baby leopard sharks look very different from adults. They have stripes and are known as zebra sharks.

MY STAR RATING

PECTORAL FIN: The broad side or pectoral fin is used mainly for steering from side to side and going up and down, rather than for pushing the shark along.

PATTERN: No one quite knows why leopard sharks have such clear markings. It could be for camouflage, or it may help them to recognize one another.

A mysterious giant of the deep, dark ocean, the megamouth was not discovered until 1976. Only one or two are seen each year, so this species may be very rare – but then, the ocean is so huge that we have no way of knowing. Like whale and basking sharks, the megamouth is a filter-feeder. The brush-like gill rakers on the sides of its head sieve tiny shrimps, fish, jellyfish and other small creatures from the sea water.

BIG MOUTH

HELLO...

Megamouths are very difficult to photograph because they usually live far below the surface, where the sea is very dark. Only about 50 have ever been seen.

NOSE: The megamouth's nose is very short, with the mouth almost at its tip, rather than being low under the head as in most other sharks.

TEETH: There are hundreds of small hooked teeth, in up to 50 rows in the upper jaw and 75 in the lower. They are not needed for feeding.

Megamouth shark

Scientific name: *Megachasma pelagios*
Shark group: Megachasmidae
Lifespan: Unknown, possibly 100 years
Length: 5.5 m
Weight: Up to 1.2 tonnes
Range: Oceans worldwide
Status: Not enough information

STAR FACT

Circular scars on the bodies of sharks such as megamouths are the result of wounds made by cookiecutter sharks. These sharp-toothed sharks feed on chunks of flesh bitten from bigger fish.

LIGHTING UP...

In some megamouths, the big, bendy, rubbery lips seem to glow in the dark. This is due to tiny light-producing organs called photophores.

MY STAR RATING

BODY: Its massive body is quite soft, tubby and flabby, and the skin is loose and dark in colour. The megamouth is not a very fast swimmer.

TAIL: The upper part (lobe) of the megamouth's tail is much longer than the lower part, in a manner similar to that of another species – the thresher shark.

The sand tiger shark's many common names include rag-tooth, snaggle-tooth and thin-tooth, as its teeth are very spiky and wide-set. It is a fearsome hunter of small fish such as herring, mackerel, flatfish and also baby sharks. The sand tiger does not mind chasing food into the shallows. This fearsome fish will even wriggle right up to where the waves lap on the beach, before turning round and splashing back into deeper water.

SNAGGLE-TOOTH

PROWL...

By day, sand tigers laze around in caves or rocky cracks. At night they come out to hunt in packs, herding fish into 'bait balls'.

STAR FACT

The sand tiger shark swallows air to alter its buoyancy (ability to float). More air inside its body makes the shark lighter, so it can stay near the surface. It then belches out the air to sink. This saves swimming energy.

SPECIAL FEATURES

TAIL: Sharks swim by swishing their tails from side to side. Although the sand tiger is a bulky, sluggish shark it can make sudden fast dashes.

REAR FINS: The two lower rear side fins, called the pelvics, help the sand tiger shark to turn sharply to the left or right.

The sand tiger has about three rows of teeth with up to 50 teeth in its upper jaw, and the same in its lower jaw.

Sand tiger shark

Scientific name: *Carcharias taurus*
Shark group: Carcharhinidae
Lifespan: 15–20 years
Length: 3 m
Weight: 150 kg
Range: Warm to tropical oceans
Status: Vulnerable

GILL SLITS: Like other sharks, the sand tiger takes in oxygen by passing water over its gills. Unusually, its gill slits are in front of its pectoral fins, and are very low.

SNOUT: Also called the grey nurse shark, the sand tiger has a streamlined narrow snout, with the mouth set some way back, below the eyes.

The whitetip reef shark spends its nights poking its nose into all kinds of cracks, crevices, holes and caves on the reef. It is looking for any prey that has tried to hide, from fish to lobsters, crabs and even octopus. Most sharks have tough skin, and the whitetip's is thick and extra-strong, to prevent scrapes and cuts as it squeezes past jagged rocks and sharp corals.

SLIM WRIGGLER

Whitetip reef shark

Scientific name: Triaenodon obesuss
Shark group: Carcharhinidae
Lifespan: 20-plus years
Length: Up to 2 m
Weight: Up to 20 kg
Range: Tropical and subtropical Indian and Pacific oceans
Status: Near threatened

AFTER YOU...

In the breeding season, whitetip reef sharks gather in shallow water to choose their partners, the males following the females.

STAR FACT

Some sharks are territorial, with a favourite place that they defend from intruders. Whitetip reef sharks have regular resting places that they may use over many years.

FIN TIPS: The whitetip is named after the pale tips on its front dorsal (back) fin and the upper end of its tail fin.

FLEXIBLE BODY: Very bendy fins and a slim, supple body allow the whitetip to squirm into very narrow gaps around the reef.

SHADY SWIMMER

Like many sharks, the bamboo shark is **nocturnal – a night-time hunter.** Like other sharks too, its camouflaging pattern tends to fade as it gets older and bigger, because fewer predators will try to attack bigger prey. Under cover of darkness on the coral reef, this slow swimmer spends its time sneaking up on many kinds of crabs, shrimps and worms, and then grabbing them with a sudden dash and bite.

SQUIRT...

Bamboo sharks have been seen squirting water at small fish hiding in rocky cracks, trying to swish them out so they can eat them.

STAR FACT

The bamboo shark is popular in aquariums because it doesn't get too big and will eat a wide range of food. Many shark species refuse food in captivity, and starve to death.

Bamboo shark

Scientific name: *Chiloscyllium punctatum*
Shark group: Hemiscylliidae
Lifespan: Unknown, possibly 15–20 years
Length: 1 m
Weight: 15 kg
Range: Southeast Asian and western Pacific coasts
Status: Near threatened

MY STAR RATING

BODY BANDS: Its horizontal bands help the young bamboo shark to merge into the shadows and moonlit patches on the reef at night.

BARBELS: Two long, thin feelers above the mouth, called barbels, help the shark feel its way by touch even in complete darkness.

The Port Jackson shark disproves the popular belief that sharks must keep swimming to stay alive. All sharks need water passing over their gills to bring continuing supplies of life-giving oxygen. But the Port Jackson shark can do this while lazing on the sea bed. The muscles in its mouth and chin make pumping movements, sucking water in through the mouth and pushing it out over the gills. Often lots of these sharks will lie in a pile on the sea bed.

SANDY SNOOZER

OUCH...

Each of its dorsal or back fins has a sharp spine at its front end, which makes the Port Jackson shark difficult for predators to swallow.

STAR FACT

If the Port Jackson shark eats something its body is unable to digest, it can turn its stomach inside out and spit it out of its mouth to get rid of the unwanted contents.

SPECIAL FEATURES

HEAD: The Port Jackson shark has a tall, wide head, large eyebrow ridges and a small mouth. It belongs to the group called the bullhead sharks.

SPIRACLES: As in a few other sharks, small openings called spiracles lie just behind each of this shark's eyes, helping the water flow for breathing.

Port Jackson shark

Scientific name: *Heterodontus portusjacksoni*
Shark group: Heterodontidae
Lifespan: Unknown, perhaps 30 years
Length: Up to 1.5 m
Weight: 15–20 kg
Range: Australian coasts
Status: Least concern

The egg cases of the Port Jackson shark have a strange corkscrew shape. This helps the eggs stay safely hidden in mud and weeds until they hatch.

FRONT TEETH: Its small, sharp front teeth are perfect for pulling little shellfish, crabs, shrimps and worms from the sea bed.

BACK TEETH: This shark's large, flat, slab-like back teeth are ideal for crushing and chewing hard-shelled foods such as mussels and clams.

Also called the puffer shark or balloon shark, the swell shark's special trick is to blow itself up! If threatened, this shark gulps water into the front part of its stomach, in the middle of its body. Doing this makes its body expand, causing it to become twice as fat as usual. It also curls itself right around and holds its tail in its mouth. It is then too big and awkward for most predators to eat. The swell shark can blow up very quickly, but it takes a while to return to its normal size.

BLOWN UP!

STAR FACT

If the swell shark is near the surface it can gulp in air to make itself swell up. When the danger is past and the shark lets out the air, it makes a barking or yapping noise, almost like a dog!

HIDE...

This shark's spots and patches provide excellent camouflage, blending with the stony sea bed, especially at night when the water is very dark.

SPECIAL FEATURES

BIG EYES: Its large, cat-like eyes have upright pupils to let in plenty of light, as the swell shark is a nocturnal hunter.

HUGE MOUTH: Almost no other shark has such a wide, huge mouth compared to its body size – not even the great white!

Swell shark

Scientific name: *Cephaloscyllium ventriosum*
Shark group: Scyliorhinidae
Lifespan: Unknown, possibly 20–30 years
Length: 1 m
Weight: 25 kg
Range: North American Pacific coasts
Status: Least concern

MERMAID'S PURSES...

Like many sharks, swell shark eggs have tough cases, called mermaid's purses. Their twirly strings hold them in the seaweed, where egg-eating animals are less likely to spot them.

SUCTION GULP: As well as lots of small sharp teeth to grab victims, the swell shark can also open its big mouth wide with sudden power to suck them in.

DENS: Each swell shark has favourite caves and cracks to rest in by day. If a predator tries to get it out, the shark swells up, becoming impossible to remove.

Big, heavy, and strong, with a mouth full of extremely sharp teeth – plus a massive appetite – few other marine creatures would tangle with a tiger shark. Without warning it will suddenly charge with lightning speed and bite hard. This makes it one of the 'Big Three' most dangerous sharks to humans, along with the great white and the bull shark. This formidable predator eats anything it can swallow – big or small, alive or dead. It is even known to be a cannibal, which means that it eats others of its own kind.

TIGER OF THE SEA

HITCHING A RIDE...

Remoras, also known as sharksucker fish, hitch rides on sharks! Using their suction fins, they attach themselves to the shark's body and get carried along. They do little lasting damage to the shark.

SPECIAL FEATURES

STRIPES: Tiger sharks are named for their markings. Their upright dark and pale stripes split and merge, just like those of real tigers.

CAMOUFLAGE: Young tiger sharks have dark stripes for camouflage in seaweed. The stripes fade as they mature and swim into the open ocean.

Sharks such as the tiger shark have a shiny reflecting layer inside the eye to catch more light, helping them to see better in gloomy night-time waters.

Tiger shark

Scientific name: *Galeocerdo cuvier*
Shark group: Carcharhinidae
Lifespan: 25-plus years
Length: 4.5 m (female larger)
Weight: Up to 650 kg
Range: Tropical and warm oceans
Status: Near threatened

STAR FACT

Tiger sharks will not only swallow almost any food. They also gulp down inedible objects such as tyres, bottles, lumps of wood and plastic, clothes, and even a musical drum.

DORSAL PIVOT: As well as helping the shark to swim straight, the dorsal (back) fin works as a pivot or swivel, which the shark swings around to change direction fast.

LIFTING FINS: Sharks tend to sink slowly as they swim, but angling the pectoral (front side) fins upwards slightly gives a lifting force to keep the nose up.

The biggest fish in the sea is also one of the most peaceful. The whale shark is larger than some types of whales, and so huge and powerful that it has little to fear – but only once it is grown up. As a baby, it's just 30–50 centimetres in length, and makes a tasty mouthful for many other kinds of sharks. Like the basking and megamouth sharks, the whale shark is a filter-feeder. Its frilly gill rakers strain small animals such as krill and baby fish from the water.

PEACEFUL GIANT

CAREFUL...

Whale sharks usually swim slowly when people are around. The main risk to human swimmers is a knock from the shark's enormous tail if it is suddenly frightened.

'STAR FACT

Whale sharks do not fear divers, and don't mind boats, unless these get too close. In fact these sharks seem to enjoy 'playing' as they twist, turn and give rides to human swimmers who pay them a visit.

SPECIAL FEATURES

MARKINGS: Each whale shark has its own pattern of spots, blotches and stripes that seem to change colour as the sun changes its angle.

RIDGES: Three raised ridges (keels) run along each side of the body. It is possible that they help water flow past the shark's body more smoothly.

Whale shark

Scientific name: *Rhincodon typus*
Shark group: Rhincodontidae
Lifespan: 70-plus years
Length: Up to 12 m
Weight: Up to 12.5 tonnes
Range: Tropical and warm oceans
Status: Vulnerable

WATCH OUT...

Whale sharks feed mainly on very small food items, little bigger than your fingers. But recent studies show they will surge at a shoal of bigger fish, open wide and gulp them in.

FEEDING: To feed without swimming, the shark sucks in water, closes its mouth and pushes the water out through its gill slits, trapping food on the rakers.

TEETH: The whale shark has hundreds of tiny teeth along its jaws, but these are not used for feeding – or for anything else, as far as we know.

It might seem like a lovely life, lazing around on the sea bed in the warm tropical shallows. This is how the wobbegong or 'wobby' goes hunting. It lies quite still, allowing its amazing camouflage to do all the work. Multicoloured flaps of skin, floppy frills and tassels hang from the wobbegong's head and body, disguising its outline so that it blends beautifully with the rocks and weeds around it. If a careless sea creature happens to swim close, the wobby leaps into action and gulps it straight down.

LAZY LIFE

OPEN WIDE...

A front view shows the wobbegong's wide mouth, frilly barbels (feelers), and the sharp, gappy teeth that ensure victims do not struggle free.

SPECIAL FEATURES

CAUDAL FIN: The lower part of the wobbegong's caudal (tail) fin is very small, so it can lie as flat as possible on the sea bed.

CAMOUFLAGE: When hunting, the wobby tries to find a patch of sea bed with the same colours as its own body, for the best camouflage.

Spotted wobbegong

Scientific name: *Orectolobus maculatus*
Shark group: Orectolobidae
Lifespan: Unknown, possibly 30-plus years
Length: Up to 3 m
Weight: Up to 100 kg
Range: Eastern Indian Ocean, around Australia
Status: Near threatened

STAR FACT

Wobbegongs have been spotted wriggling and hauling themselves across seashore rocks to get back into the ocean, usually after being trapped in a rock pool by the falling tide.

KEEP LOW...

The wobbegong is a member of the carpet shark group. Its body is flattened from the top to underside, so it lies better on the sea bed.

MY STAR RATING

SUCKING POWER: The wobbegong opens its mouth wide with such power that water is sucked in with great force – carrying nearby prey along with it.

WHISKERS: Small string-like barbels and tassels hang around the wobby's mouth and wave in the current, attracting curious creatures for lunch.

Few other sea creatures can escape a shortfin mako when this shark is swimming at full speed. Smooth and super-streamlined, it dashes after tuna, bluefish and even swordfish, which are themselves among the champion speedy swimmers. The mako can also twist and swerve faster than the human eye can follow. Once its sharp, curved teeth jab into flesh and its jaws get a good grip, the quarry is dead meat.

RAPID STRIKE

Shortfin mako

Scientific name: *Isurus oxyrinchus*
Shark group: Lamnidae
Lifespan: Unclear, perhaps 20–25 years
Length: Usually up to 3 m
Weight: Varies widely, 150–400 kg
Range: Tropical to cool oceans
Status: Vulnerable

STAR FACT

There's no quicker shark than the shortfin mako. It can race along in sudden short bursts at more than 70 km/h. This puts it among the top ten fastest fish in the sea.

WOW...

Sharks have tiny ampullae (pits) on their head and snouts. These detect natural electrical pulses given off by the muscles of other animals.

MY STAR RATING

SPECIAL FEATURES

TEETH: Sharks grow new teeth continually at the back of the jaw. These move forwards slowly for use. This mako has three rows of working teeth.

LEAPING: The mako can escape danger, such as a bigger shark, by leaping clear of the water – as high as 7 m above the surface.

INDEX

Entries in **bold** refer to main subject entries, which are always illustrated.

G

H

I

J

K

L

M

N

O

P

ACKNOWLEDGEMENTS

The publishers would like to thank the following sources for the use of their photographs:

Key (m) = main (i) = inset (c) = card

Page 9 Rolf Nussbaumer/naturepl.com
Grey wolf (m) Laurent Geslin/naturepl.com, (i/c) Tim Fitzharris/Minden Pictures/FLPA
Rock python (m/c) Bruce Davidson/naturepl.com, (i) Peter Blackwell/naturepl.com
Killer whale (m) Brandon Cole/naturepl.com, (i/c) Hiroya Minakuchi/Minden Pictures/FLPA
Tiger (m) Anup Shah/naturepl.com, (i/c) Tim Fitzharris/Minden Pictures/FLPA
Eagle owl (m/c) Juniors Bildarchiv/Photolibrary.com, (i) Malcolm Schuyl/FLPA
Barracuda (m/c) Jeff Rotman/naturepl.com
Red-bellied piranha (m/c) Pete Oxford/naturepl.com
Nile crocodile (m) Anup Shah/naturepl.com, (i/c) Vincent Grafhorst/Minden Pictures/FLPA
Huntsman spider (m/c) Gerry Ellis/Minden Pictures/FLPA, (i) Nick Garbutt/naturepl.com
Polar bear (m/c) Rob Reijnen/Minden Pictures/FLPA, (i) T.J. Rich/naturepl.com
Golden eagle (m) Malcolm Schuyl/FLPA, (i/c) Malcolm Schuyl/FLPA
Solifuge (m) Mark Moffett/Minden Pictures/FLPA, (i/c) Piotr Naskrecki/Minden Pictures/FLPA
Horned frog (m/c) Pete Oxford/naturepl.com
Eyelash viper (m/c) David A. Northcott/Corbis
Spotted hyaena (m) Andrew Parkinson/naturepl.com, (i/c) Hermann Brehm/naturepl.com
Leopard seal (m/c) Paul Nicklen/Getty Images, (i) Tui De Roy/Minden Pictures/FLPA
Praying mantis (m/c) Michael & Patricia Fogden/ Minden Pictures/FLPA, (i) Preston-Mafham/ Premaphotos/naturepl
African wild dog (m) Bruce Davidson/naturepl.com, (i/c) ImageBroker/Imagebroker/FLPA
Gannet (m) Paul Hobson/FLPA (i) Gianpiero Ferrari/FLPA
Least weasel (m/c) Flip De Nooyer/FN/Minden/FLPA

Page 45 John Mitchell/Photolibrary.com
Sailfish (m/c) Doug Perrine/naturepl.com, (i) Doug Perrine/naturepl.com
Giraffe (m) Martin Harvey/Corbis, (i/c) Frans Lanting/FLPA
Peregrine falcon (m/c) Imagebroker/FLPA, (i) Mark Payne-Gill/naturepl.com
Elephant seal (m/c) Flip Nicklin/Minden Pictures/ FLPA, (i) Ingo Arndt/naturepl.com
Black-throated hummingbird (m/c) Kim Taylor/ naturepl.com, (i) Tom Vezo/naturepl.com
Stonefish (m/c) Georgette Douwma/naturepl.com
Sunfish (m/c) Hiroya Minakuchi/Minden Pictures/FLPA
Emperor penguin (m) Fritz Poelking/Photolibrary.com, (i/c) Rob Reijnen/Minden Pictures/FLPA
Army ant (m/c) Piotr Naskrecki/Minden Pictures/ FLPA, (i) Mark Moffett/Minden Pictures/FLPA
Ostrich (m) Michael Krabs/Photolibrary.com, (i/c) Jurgen & Christine Sohns/FLPA
Cheetah (m/c) Winfried Wisniewski/FN/Minden/FLPA, (i) Richard Du Toit/naturepl.com
Sperm whale (m/c) Brandon Cole/naturepl.com, (i) Flip Nicklin/Minden Pictures/FLPA
Spectacled fruit bat (m/c) Theo Allofs/Minden Pictures/FLPA
Arctic tern (m/c) Winfried Wisniewski/Minden Pictures/FLPA
Japanese macaque (m) Ingo Arndt/naturepl.com, (i/c) Dickie Duckett/FLPA
Lesser flamingo (m/c) Anup Shah/naturepl.com, (i) Anup Shah/naturepl.com
Star-nosed mole (m/c) Dembinsky Photo Ass./FLPA, (i) Breck P Kent/Photolibrary.com
Galapagos marine iguana (m) Tui De Roy/ Minden Pictures/FLPA, (i/c) Michio Hoshino/Minden Pictures/FLPA
Steller's sea eagle (m/c) Sergey Gorshkov/Minden Pictures/FLPA, (i) Kerstin Hinze/naturepl.com
Pale-throated sloth (m/c) Staffan Widstrand/ naturepl.com

Page 81 Barry Mansell/Photolibrary.com
Jackson's chameleon (m/c) Corbis/Photolibrary.com, (i) Solvin Zankl/naturepl.com
Porcupine fish (m/c) J. W. Alker/Imagebroker/FLPA, (i) Norbert Probst/Imagebroker/FLPA
Aardvark (m) Frans Lanting/FLPA, (i/c) Owen Newman/naturepl.com
Peacock mantis shrimp (m/c) Chris Newbert/FLPA, (i) Solvin Zankl/naturepl.com
Short-beaked echidna (m) Cyril Ruoso/FLPA, (i/c) Steven David Miller/naturepl.com
Goldenrod crab spider (m/c) Nick Garbutt/ naturepl.com
Giraffe weevil (m/c) Michael Krabs/Imagebroker/FLPA
Knobbed hornbill (m) Tui De Roy/FLPA, (i/c) Tim Laman/naturepl.com
Frilled lizard (m/c) Michael & Patricia Fogden/FLPA, (i) ANT Photo Library/NHPA
Vampire bat (m/c) Michael & Patricia Fogden/FLPA, (i) Jim Clare/naturepl.com
Platypus (m) Dave Watts/naturepl.com, (i/c) Dave Watts/naturepl.com
Three-banded armadillo (m/c) Mark Payne-Gill/ naturepl.com (i) Mark Payne-Gill/naturepl.com
Pot-belly seahorse (m/c) George Grall/Getty Images
Tyron's sea slug (m/c) Colin Marshall/FLPA
Naked mole rat (m/c) Raymond Mendez/ Photolibrary.com, (i) Neil Bromhall/naturepl.com
Ecuador tree frog (m/c) Pete Oxford/FLPA (i) Pete Oxford/FLPA
Tuatara (m/c) Pete Oxford/naturepl.com, (i) Mark Moffett/FLPA
Hoatzin (m) Pete Oxford/naturepl.com, (i/c) Flip De Nooyer/FLPA
Stalk-eyed fly (m) Mark Moffett/FLPA, (i/c) Phil Savoie/naturepl.com
Proboscis monkey (m/c) Nick Garbutt/naturepl.com

Page 117 moodboard RF/Photolibrary.com
African elephant (m/c) Karl Ammann/naturepl.com, (i) Anup Shah/naturepl.com
Green anaconda (m/c) Ingo Arndt/Minden Pictures/FLPA, (i) Luiz Claudio Marigo/naturepl.com
Blue whale (m/c) Flip Nicklin/Minden Pictures/FLPA, (i) Mark Carwardine/naturepl.com
Giant anteater (m) Morales Morales/Photolibrary.com, (i/c) Pete Oxford/naturepl.com
Galapagos giant tortoise (m/c) Mark Moffett/ Minden Pictures/FLPA (i) Andy Rouse/naturepl.com
Goliath bird-eating spider (m/c) Rod Williams/ naturepl.com
Japanese giant hornet (m/c) Alastair MacEwen/ Photolibrary.com
Giant otter (m/c) Fritz Polking/FLPA, (i) Luiz Claudio Marigo/naturepl.com
Giant grouper (m/c) Norbert Wu/Minden Pictures/ FLPA, (i) Jurgen Freund/naturepl.com
Hippopotamus (m) Juniors Bildarchiv/ Photolibrary.com, (i/c) Tony Heald/naturepl.com
Komodo dragon (m/c) R.Dirscherl/FLPA, (i) Reinhard Dirscherl/FLPA
Lion's mane jellyfish (m/c) Scott Leslie/Minden Pictures/FLPA, (i) ImageBroker/FLPA
Giant coconut crab (m/c) Ariadne Van Zandbergen/ FLPA
Bison (m/c) ImageBroker/FLPA
Mountain gorilla (m) Thomas Marent/Minden Pictures/FLPA, (i) Andy Rouse/naturepl.com
Wandering albatross (m/c) Ben Osborne/ Photolibrary.com, (i) Ian McCarthy/naturepl.com
Saltwater crocodile (m/c) Tom and Pam Gardner/ FLPA, (i) Reinhard Dirscherl/FLPA
Manta ray (m/c) Jens Kuhfs/Getty Images/ Photolibrary.com, (i) Brandon Cole/naturepl.com
Giant African land snail (m/c) Vincent Grafhorst/ Minden Pictures/FLPA, (i) Martin B Withers/FLPA
Pacific giant octopus (m/c) David Fleetham/ naturepl.com

Page 153 Dan Burton/naturepl.com
Basking shark (m/c) Dan Burton/naturepl.com, (i) Chris Gomersall/naturepl.com
Blue shark (m/c) Tobias Bernhard/Photolibrary.com, (i) Richard Herrmann/Photolibrary.com
Great white shark (m/c) Mike Parry/Minden Pictures/FLPA, (i) Tony Heald/naturepl.com
Greenland shark (m) Doug Perrine/naturepl.com, (i/c) Doug Perrine/naturepl.com
Bull shark (m) Brandon Cole/naturepl.com, (i/c) Brandon Cole/naturepl.com
Spiny dogfish (m/c) Seapics.com
Pacific angel shark (m/c) Flip Nicklin/Minden Pictures/FLPA
Scalloped hammerhead shark (m/c) Doug Perrine/ naturepl.com, (i) Chris Newbert/Minden Pictures/ FLPA
Lemon shark (m) Jeff Rotman/naturepl.com, (i/c) Brandon Cole/naturepl.com
Leopard shark (m/c) R.Dirscherl/FLPA, (i) Jurgen Freund/naturepl.com
Megamouth shark (m/c) Bruce Rasner/Rotman/ naturepl.com, (i) Seapics.com
Sand tiger shark (m) Doug Perrine/naturepl.com, (i/c) Norbert Wu/Minden Pictures/FLPA
Whitetip reef shark (m/c) Norbert Wu/Minden Pictures/FLPA
Bamboo shark (m/c) Doug Perrine/naturepl.com
Port Jackson shark (m/c) Fred Bavendam/Minden Pictures/FLPA, (i) Fred Bavendam/Minden Pictures/ FLPA
Swell shark (m/c) Norbert Wu/Minden Pictures/FLPA, (i) Flip Nicklin/Minden Pictures/FLPA
Tiger shark (m) Norbert Wu/Minden Pictures/FLPA, (i/c) Michael Pitts/naturepl.com
Whale shark (m) James Watt/Photolibrary.com, (i/c) Flip Nicklin/Minden Pictures/FLPA
Spotted wobbegong (m/c) Fred Bavendam/Minden Pictures/FLPA, (i) Chris Newbert/Minden Pictures/ FLPA
Shortfin mako (m/c) Chris and Monique Fallows/ Photolibrary.com

Every effort has been made to acknowledge the source and copyright holder of each picture. Miles Kelly Publishing apologises for any unintentional errors or omissions.